AF577104

Dedication:

Some may think that the mountains were made for the tourists, a roadside attraction of magnificent proportions. Perhaps the tourists were made for the mountains, as audience to a sublime performance. Actually, we are all visitors in the mountain wilderness, only our length of stay varies. This book is about mountains and tourists. It is dedicated to those who come to look, and leave a little behind.

LEGACY IN ICE

GLACIER HOUSE

GLACIER, B. C.

A Glimpse of the Canadian Alps.

Within ~~less than two decades~~ only a dozen years there has been ~~open~~ made accessible to the lover of Nature, a district in the British possessions, lying just beyond our northern border, ~~a district~~ which for scenic ~~beauty~~ grandeur & beauty is without a rival ~~on~~ the American continent, & possibly unsurpassed anywhere.

Prior to the opening of the Canadian Pacific Railway the Canadian Alps were an unknown wilderness. True the Hudson's Bay & Northwest Fur Trading Companies' posts were scattered over the Country, but in the main

Notes for an article by George Vaux, *ca* 1899.

LEGACY IN ICE The Vaux Family and the Canadian Alps

Edward Cavell

The Whyte Foundation, Banff, Alberta, Canada.

THE VAUX FAMILY AND THE CANADIAN ALPS

George Vaux Sr. and his children, Mary, George Jr., and William Jr., saw the mountains of western Canada for the first time in 1887, while travelling on the recently completed Canadian Pacific Railway, and "that was it for them." For the next forty years various members of the family would spend most of their free time in the Rocky and Selkirk mountain ranges. Together, as talented amateur artists and scientists, they made a lasting contribution to the mountains of Canada.

The Vaux (pronounced vox) family arrived at the newly-opened Glacier House Hotel at the foot of the immense Great Glacier on July 15, 1887. The next day they went to the toe of the glacier, a moderately easy one-and-one-half mile walk over a rough trail. They took a few photographs, enjoyed the view of the magnificent Selkirk Mountains, then proceeded on to Banff before returning home to Philadelphia, Pennsylvania.

Their innocent "snapshots" were the earliest known photographs of the Great Glacier of the Illecillewaet at its modern climax. The recognition of this, a few years later, immersed the family in a life-long study of glaciers and the mountain environment, the first formal study of glaciers in Canada. George and William Vaux Jr. delivered numerous papers, monographs and pamphlets before organizations such as the Academy of Natural Sciences of Philadelphia, and were published in a number of journals. Illustrated lectures all three of the "children" gave helped to kindle and fuel what William Vaux Jr. referred to as a "decided Rocky Mountain cult," which was developing in the eastern United States. Their photographic legacy is the essence of the duality of art and science.

The Vaux family could hardly be considered as average tourists by today's standards. Advantaged, well-educated Quakers, they were the epitome of the well-rounded Victorian; committed, inquisitive, and dedicated to the advancement of man's understanding and appreciation of nature.

Camp at Lake Marion, July 28, 1897.
George Vaux Jr. far left, Sam Youwell, J.H. Stallard, Mary Vaux and Mrs. Stallard in left part of tent entrance.

Talented amateur artists and scientists, they fell under the spell of the Canadian Alps. What George Jr. described as "the consciousness that so little exploration has been carried out that each visitor is practically a new discoverer" spurred their dedication and commitment.

The family's first visit in 1887 was part of a quick return trip east after vacationing in the western United States, their curiosity having been piqued by the opening of the Canadian Pacific Railway the previous year. The railway had been officially completed in the fall of 1885 but additional work delayed the inauguration of the first transcontinental passenger train until July of 1886. The Vauxes' earnest commitment to the mountains began in 1894 when they returned to stay for a month, spending slightly more than a week at each of the featured mountain centres of Banff, Lake Louise and Glacier. It was then that they noted the retreat of the Illecillewaet Glacier. They became fascinated by glacial phenomena and spent a considerable amount of time photographing the many unique ice features.

In 1897, returning to spend two weeks at Glacier House, they met Dr. J.H. Stallard and his wife, regular visitors to the Selkirks. The Stallards, experienced mountaineers, introduced the young Vauxes to mountain climbing. For the first time the family visited the more easily accessible high points around Glacier House, climbing Mount Abbott and crossing the Asulkan Glacier to the spectacular Asulkan Pass. They also met Edward J. Duschesnay, the CPR assistant-general superintendent, who was to become a close friend and a supporter of their glacial studies.

Their activities in the Selkirks from 1897 on are recorded, in part, in a register kept at Glacier House which this publication reproduces in part. This *Scrapbook* documents the fascination of the Victorian traveller, including the Vaux family, with the virgin mountains of the Selkirk Range, and demonstrates the growing involvement of the urban population with the wilderness.

William did considerable research on glaciers over the winter of 1897; when the family returned in 1898 they began their work in earnest. They studied both the Illecillewaet and Asulkan Glaciers in much greater detail and standardized their measuring technique. When they departed after a three week stay, they left some of their mountaineering and photographic developing equipment in the care of Miss Mollison, the manager of Glacier House. The Vaux family was coming back! That winter George and William Jr. wrote their first paper on their glacier studies and presented it before the Academy of Natural Sciences.

The family soon established a routine for the summers' activities. Mary would spend most of the summer in the Rockies with her father, George Sr., George Jr. and William Jr. would visit as their ever increasing business schedule would allow. Summers they spent in the mountains; winters they dreamt about them, preparing presentations on their glacier work, or giving electric lantern shows (the precursor of the 35mm slide show). Mary may have expressed their frustrations when she wrote in 1912:

Sometimes I feel that I can hardly wait till the time comes to escape from city life to the free air of the everlasting hills. I sometimes wonder how it is that those who love the out of doors so much, seem always to have their lots cast in the manmade town.

Once they completed their initial surveys it took less time each year to maintain the study. After 1899 the family extended its area of activity, spending more time in the Yoho Valley and the Lake Louise district, making occasional side trips to places like Bow Lake and Mount Assiniboine. The family assiduously avoided Banff, George Jr. writing:

The consensus of opinion of those best qualified to judge is that the attractions are far inferior to those several points a little further west. Banff has more of the attributes of a summer watering place, whilst at the others there is less formality and an opportunity to get closer to nature.

Banff Avenue, the main street in Banff, July 5, 1894.

The Family

The Vaux family was very much a product of its time and milieu. Philadelphia was America's second largest city and a dominant centre of commerce. Institutions like the American Philosophical Society, the Franklin Institute and the Academy of Natural Sciences created for the city its reputation as a centre of learning and culture. Inventions and advancements like Bell's telephone, Edison's light bulb, and the internal combustion engine helped to make the late Victorian age a technological wonderland. "Civilization" was advancing at an unheard of rate. The American wilderness was rapidly being consumed and bound by the railways. Society was more mobile than ever before, expanding settlement and commerce and creating the ubiquitous tourist. The concept of travel for recreation entered the world.

It was also the age of the amateur; originally defined as one who pursues an interest simply for the love of it, the term lacked negative connotations. Intelligent, inquisitive minds were encouraged to create; it was considered one of man's highest functions—if not duty—to contribute in any way possible to his society. With so much of the modern world still to discover, important contributions did not depend on an overwhelming level of technical support and academic background.

Several emerging art forms such as photography, and the newer earth sciences were very much the amateur's domain. Simple experiment and observation techniques could lead to important advancements. William Vaux wrote of his Canadian glacial studies that: "...everything is so new and unknown the investigations will become doubly valuable from a scientific standpoint, and the student will have the satisfaction of knowing that he is treading in steps but seldom attempted by others...." The air of discovery, of fact as well as untrod landscapes, permeated Victorian society with the excitement of exploration and the belief of personal contribution.

As affluent, well educated and active citizens of Philadelphia the Vaux family was part of the mainstream of society, with all the drives and expectations of the Victorian privileged class. The Vauxes were proud of their heritage, which traced English-Norman ancestors to James and Richard Vaux, who arrived in America in the mid-18th century. In proverbial colonial American style, James Vaux played host to George Washington (and the next night his adversary, General Howe) at his farm near Valley Forge. Being Quakers, however, instilled a "sense of difference" that kept them aloof from many aspects of this society.

The Quakers arrived in America in the late 17th century. Offshoots and dissenters from the Puritan movement in England, they were strong in their Christian faith; the belief that "there is that of God in every man" led to the testimonies of pacifism, simplicity, community and equality which are the Quaker essence. Their "Rules of Discipline" advocate simplicity in dress, lifestyle and speech ("Thee" was traditionally used to protest the social stratification created by the use of the plural and formal term "you"). Days and months were numbered rather than using "pagan" words like "Sunday" or "October." The Friends "meetings" (an equivalent to church services), the technique of silent worship, and the use of a lay clergy created a powerful sense of community and collective spirit in the Religious Society of Friends. Children were given a "guarded" education in schools operated by the Society which stressed the testimonies and the "Rules of Discipline."

Pastimes like dancing, music, gambling and theatre were considered "vain sports" and the intemperate use of alcohol an "unnatural" activity (much to the displeasure of some of the mountain guides and packers who worked for Quakers). The "fear of airy notions" led to an intrinsic distrust of art and literature. The more practical pursuits of engineering, law, medicine and science were stressed, the reading of histories, biographies and travel accounts preferred over fiction (or political) prose. The strong sense of commitment and community felt by the Friends resulted in a long tradition of humanitarian activities. Native rights, penal reform, civil liberties and the peace movement have all continued to profit by their often quiet but strong support.

Vaux party departing for a ride, Lake Louise Chalet, 1906.

Throughout the 19th century their tradition of hard work and sound business practices led to a general prosperity among the Quakers. The natural proclivities towards creature comforts and possessions and the pressures exerted by the predominate American society caused the Quakers to be indistinguishable from the rest of the American middle class. The relaxing of the testimony regarding simple dress resulted in the loss of the traditional "cereal box" image. The latter part of the century saw major liberalizing influences throughout the Society, but traditional Quaker values were maintained.

The Vauxes, as one of the oldest and most prominent Philadelphian Quaker families, was very involved in the activities of the Society of Friends. George Vaux Sr. was considered an authority on Quaker history and participated in many of the Society's humanitarian aid programs. His children, Mary, George Jr., and William Jr., all received guarded educations at Quaker schools and were deeply committed to the Society of Friends. Their interests and activities, however, place them among the more liberal elements of the Society.

The patriarch of the family, George Vaux Sr. (1832-1915), was an autocratic man who was a powerful influence over his children throughout his life, despite their own coming of age. Both George Sr. and his brother William Sr. were "men of affairs" with business interests throughout Pennsylvania. William S. Vaux Sr. (1811-1882) was an eclectic collector of things as diverse as coins and native artifacts. A dedicated mineralogist, he travelled extensively in Europe and America on collecting trips. An avid supporter of the Academy of Natural Sciences, he held a number of positions on its executive board. The collection of minerals he bequeathed to the Academy was considered to be the largest of its kind in America.
His involvement in the natural sciences was an important influence on the Vaux children.
The medicinal properties of mountain air and the fact that George Sr. "enjoyed ill health" were probably initially responsible for the annual return of the Vaux clan, but it was William Sr. who gave direction to their involvement.

The mountains were the family's common work ground, their love of wilderness a uniting force. Despite their close family ties and unified public image, created through their shared credit on publications and exhibitions, each member of the family was an individual with separate interests and diverse approaches to the mountains.

William S. Vaux Jr. (1872-1908), the youngest of the family, died of tuberculosis at thirty-six, "caught while eating in the hash houses near his building projects." His abbreviated life may have limited the quantity of his contribution but not the quality.

He graduated, in 1893, from Haverford College (a Quaker school) with a B.Sc. in engineering and worked as an architect in Philadelphia, specializing in structural engineering. It was his fascination with glaciers, his drive and technical ability that caused the family to start on the glacial studies. All of the articles, monographs and booklets were basically by William with some assistance from his brother. George Jr. wrote about the glacial studies after William's death in 1908:

It was his enthusiasm and love of nature which caused us first to enter upon them; he it was who had given most of the thought and study to the subject, who had done the larger part of the instrumental work, and all of the final reductions of the observations, in order to secure results. Hence it is that the writer finds himself at considerable disadvantage in continuing the observations and the reports upon them.

William's diaries, kept while in the mountains, are the basis for most of the glacier articles. Filled with meticulous notes in his neat hand, they contain measurements, sketches and observations of the glaciers as well as descriptions and accounts of his various mountain travels. Occasionally his usually straightforward entries are interrupted with more personal notes: Edward Whymper, the famous climber, was "a little off-colour... most of the time;" Mary Schäffer, a family friend and soon-to-become-famous explorer, was "terrified at the early rise and did not get up."

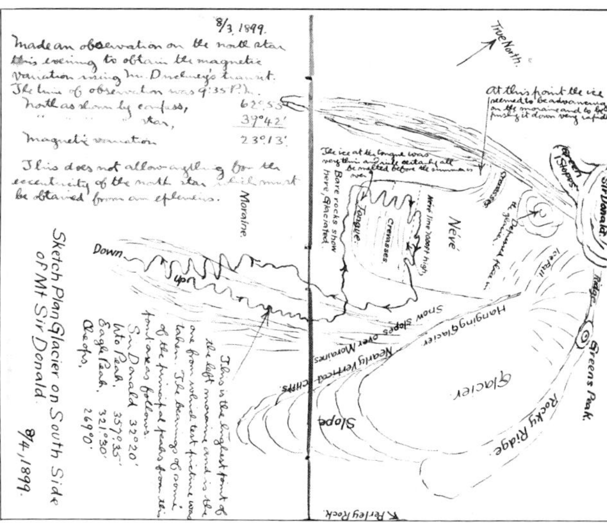

Diary page, William S. Vaux Jr.

By 1898 he had already developed a rather possessive attitude towards the mountains, and obviously felt that he had lost his tourist standing. An article published in the *Minneapolis Journal* states that:

Mr. Vaux can not understand the ignorance and indifference to this wonderful mountain region which he finds throughout the west . . . . The attitude of the people who do visit the magnificent portion of the mountains is also an irritation to all enthusiastic mountain lovers, such as he. They generally stop over one night and walk up to the foot of the Great Glacier, stroll around the hotel, feeling that they have done all that there is to do.

In his obituary his brother says of him that: "Whilst not lacking in artistic feeling, he devoted his energy largely to the practical side of his subject." William's engineering background is evident in the articles he wrote and the pictures he took. *The Canadian Pacific from Laggan to Revelstoke* B.C., one of his most ambitious papers, is an in-depth account of the structural features of the line. He describes, in great detail, bridge construction, hydraulic grading, the dangers of avalanches, and the necessity and structure of snowsheds, but he barely mentions the scenery. A large portion of the photographs in the collection reflects his reverence for technology, as he appears to have taken most of the pictures of railway structures and equipment.

His major paper *Modern Glaciers* was written for the Engineers' Club of Philadelphia just before his death. It is the culmination of all his glacier work. A detailed, clear, and carefully written description of the nature of glaciers along with an overview of the history of the study of glaciers and an account of the family's work in the Canadian mountains, the paper is indicative of the level of dedication William applied to the study and was so well received that it was republished in both *Appalachia* and the *Canadian Alpine Journal*.

A member of the Alpine Club of Canada and founding member and treasurer of the American Alpine Club, William was an active outdoorsman but, not a climber, he refrained from major ascents, preferring to work on the glaciers. A description in his diary of one early morning start for a hike to the Asulkan Glacier gives a good impression of his appreciation of the mountains. They started at 4 a.m:

Just as we left the Chalet [Glacier House] the sun began to tip the higher peaks with light and as we followed the path lined on both sides with ferns, moss and blueberry bushes, the air full of the delicious odor of the forest, and our eyes feasted on the wonderful harmony of light and shade. We could not but congratulate ourselves on our early start and I wonder why it was that people who make believe to be lovers of nature, sleep away the time when nature shows itself in its most bewitching moods."

William's diaries and descriptions of him written after his death give us an image of an amiable but slightly shy man who pursued his interests with great energy. Though hardly shirking public duties, William, out of reticence, or possibly his respect for seniority, deferred to his brother George Jr. in most public presentations.

George Vaux Jr. (1863-1927) once described the Rocky Mountains as "cold, severe, beautiful, grand, unapproachably majestic," a view of the mountains that indicates a different approach from the single-minded pursuit of glaciers his brother indulged in. Though he spent a considerable amount of time assisting William with the glacier measurements, he was more likely to wander off with sister Mary in search of high places and scenic wonder. He was also apt to be more reflective about the mountains:

When this view [Lake Louise] is seen in the early dawn, the entrancing beauty enhanced by a flood of rosy light, & the whole mirrored perfectly in the placid waters of the unruffled lake, words convey no idea of its loveliness & imagination can fire but slight idea to one who has never seen for himself & had his thoughts turned upward by the sight.

Hydraulic grading, Mountain Creek, Selkirks, Aug. 8, 1899.

William and George Vaux Jr. by a crevasse, 1906.

George was born in 1863, graduated from Haverford College and received an LL.B. from the University of Pennsylvania in 1888. He was admitted to the bar and eventually worked in corporate and estate law. He gained an extensive reputation for his penal reform work as an inspector of the Eastern State Penitentary and for his work with the Philadelphia House of Refuge, the Institute for Colored Youth and many other Quaker benevolent and educational institutions.

From 1906 until his death he was a member, and chairman from 1912, of the United States Board of Indian Commissioners. A watchdog organization over the Bureau of Indian Affairs, the commission was responsible for overseeing all transactions between the government and native peoples. From its inception in 1869 the board traditionally had two Quakers as members, in recognition of the extensive involvement of the Society of Friends in the welfare of American Indians. George was a very active member of the board and was responsible for a number of beneficial changes in the treatment of the Indians. His work for the board involved extensive travel to a number of reservations throughout the United States. These new duties were partially responsible for his not returning to the Canadian Rockies after 1911.

At forty-four George was the first of the Vaux "children" to marry. He had met his wife, Mary James (another Mary Vaux to carry on the family propensity of repeating names), while in the Rockies in 1905. Sons George Jr. and Henry, born in 1908 and 1912 respectively, are the only progeny of this generation of the Vaux family.

George Vaux Jr. was active in a number of Philadelphian societies, principally the Academy of Natural Sciences, the Photographic Society and the Mineralogical Society, for all of which he held a number of executive positions. His consuming interest, however, was mineralogy. Influenced by William Vaux Sr., George dedicated a considerable amount of time and expense to building a collection of minerals that eventually rivalled his uncle's. Though unable to participate, he co-sponsored, with the Academy of Natural Sciences, a number of collecting expeditions to Greenland, South Africa and South America. On one expedition to Bolivia a new specimen was named Vauxite in his honour. His collection of over ten thousand specimens is now at Bryn Mawr College.

Out of a sense of competition and aware of maintaining the family's list of firsts, he was not above photographic one-upmanship. Sir James Outram met George, Mary and Mr. Duschesnay at Twin Falls in the Yoho Valley:

Mr. Vaux was much elated at being five minutes ahead of me and the first to take a near photograph of the Twins. Mr. Wilcox had been there earlier, but one of the streams was indisposed, suffering from a landslide in its upper channel, and refused to work. So Mr. Duschesnay, with his usual readiness and thoughtfulness, had despatched the workmen to remove the obstruction, and this was the first appearance of the invalid since his illness.

The cure for the invalid was a healthy charge of dynamite. It was not the first time the CPR had improved the scenery.

George Jr. was an avid outdoorsman and, like his siblings, a founding member of the Canadian and American Alpine Clubs and a member of the Appalachian Mountain Club. He was a more active climber and more interested in general scenic photography than his brother. In 1900 he became the first American and the first "amateur" to climb Mount Sir Donald, only the third ascent of the highest peak in the Glacier House area. He was "assisted up the mountain" by Edouard Feuz and Christian Häsler, the Swiss guides who had been imported by the CPR in 1899. The sixteen hour climb was enlivened by an electrical storm on the summit:

Each shrill crack of thunder would be preceded by a sharp buzzing from the points of our ice axes . . . . It was necessary to beat a hasty retreat amidst the appalling surroundings. Prudence compelled us to take shelter under an overhanging cliff to gain protection from the ice and stones which soon began to fall, loosened by the rain and wind.

Twin Falls, Yoho Valley, British Columbia, Aug. 18, 1901.

A few days later George and his sister Mary climbed Mount Stephen near Field, again with Häsler and Feuz. From the summit of Mount Stephen they saw the Wapta Fall (Takakkaw Falls) in the Yoho Valley and it "whetted our appetites for what we should find on a closer acquaintance." In 1900 the Yoho Valley (then called the North Fork Valley) had seen very little activity. Jean Habel had first explored it in 1896 at the urging of Tom Wilson, but it wasn't until that summer that anything approaching tourist trails were built past Emerald Lake. On August 26, 1900, the entire family, including George Sr., with Christian Häsler as guide, travelled over Yoho Pass to photograph Takakkaw Falls. This was an important moment for Mary, as she later wrote to Dr. Charles Walcott:

"Thee knows I feel a sense of ownership in it (the Yoho Valley), being the first white woman that visited it . . . . It is to me the loveliest spot to be found, and it always quickens my blood when I hear and speak of it. I can imagine no greater delight than camping there away from the tourist, and the noise of the iron horse."

Mary M. Vaux (1860-1940) was the eldest of the three children and had the longest involvement in the "Canadian Alps," returning annually until 1939. She received the standard "guarded" education at the Friends Select School, graduating in 1879. She also received good grounding in drawing and watercolour painting from a private tutor. Quakers were among the most progressive groups with respect to women's rights, but Mary was still bound by many of the social limitations of the nineteenth century. Unlike her brothers, she did not receive a post-secondary education; she was neither expected to nor did she establish a business career. To her lot fell the more traditional roles of women. Mary's mother, Sarah Vaux, died the same year Mary graduated from school, leaving her with the responsibility of keeping house for her father and brothers at both the family home on Arch Street and the summer place at Bryn Mawr. She also ran the dairy farm that was part of the Bryn Mawr estate.

Mary garnered a number of firsts in the mountains of which she was duly proud—first woman in the Yoho Valley, first over 10,000 feet (on Mount Stephen), and first over Abbot Pass at Lake Louise. Along with her close friend, Mary Schäffer, she was the first woman to explore the Deutschman Caves, discovered near Glacier in 1905. Mary Schäffer, who was to do extensive explorations in what was to become Jasper National Park, named Mount Mary Vaux, a prominent peak at Maligne Lake, for her. (Mount Vaux, near Field, was named by Sir James Hector for a distant English relative of the family).

Mary's involvement with the Yoho area was to become very extensive. She made a complete high circuit of the valley over the glaciers and snowfields from Sherbrooke Lake to the Little Yoho Valley. She camped in and explored all parts of the valley as well as carrying out measurements of the Yoho Glacier. As another first, she made the approach to the valley from Bow Glacier by Vulture Col, and Balfour and Yoho Glaciers with a small Alpine Club of Canada group. It was on this trip in 1910, with A.O. Wheeler, Dr. Longstaff, Byron Harmon and others, that she proved herself to be an old hand at mountain travel, comfortable in the ways of camp life: "Miss Vaux, in some magical way, had managed to conjure from the wilderness two fat and tender turkeys, one of which formed the pièce de resistance of that evening's sumptuous feast." Veteran status was conferred on Mary once more in the same article in the *Canadian Alpine Journal*:

A transcontinental train was in the station as we filed past and our cortège seemed to afford as much astonishment and speculation as did the arrival of Tartarin in the lobby of the Rigi-Kulm. Miss Vaux, in buckskin shirt and knickerbockers, went over to the office to post a letter, and was snap-shotted without mercy . . . .

Mary assisted in the early glacial studies and took them over completely after 1911, continuing them sporadically until 1922. She gave lantern slide lectures on mountain themes in and around Philadelphia, as well as writing a number of articles.

The Yoho Valley from summit of Mount Stephen, July 21, 1900.

An overenthusiastic article in the Banff newspaper, the *Crag and Canyon*, refers to her as: "Miss Mary Vaux, who has done more to advertise the Canadian Rockies by magazine articles and photographs than perhaps any other living writer."

Mary didn't write about glaciers until after 1910, leaving that to her brothers. Instead she described travel and camp life and the mountains in general. In an unpublished manuscript she describes an aspect of camp life at Lake O'Hara near Lake Louise:

Our camp had one disadvantage—the porcupines. They seemed so pleased to have us & visited us at all hours; tried the flavor of our bacon, & the softness of the guides' bed in their tent. When they found we did not encourage greater intimacy they climbed the large tree immediately back of the tent, & watched us from this point of vantage all day. Then at night they would scratch on the canvas just by our heads & grunt in the most impudent manner. Christian killed one with his ice axe, as he filled the guides blankets with quills & would not come out of their tent. We would have eaten him but Dan did not understand how to prepare him for the table, & he looked so formidable in his spiny coat."

Mary spent virtually every summer in the Rockies for over forty years, making many friends and becoming somewhat the "Grand Dame" of the mountains. A respected perennial at Alpine Club camps, she was referred to as "the Artist." She was once described as having the "simplicity and näiveté of a child, with the business astuteness and driving force of a master of men. Entirely self-reliant, she drew people to her by the force of her independence and character."

In 1914, at fifty-four, Mary married Dr. Charles Doolittle Walcott (1850-1927), secretary of the Smithsonian Institution in Washington, D.C., a noted geologist and invertebrate paleontologist. They met while Dr. Walcott was camped near Field, working on what could be considered his most important discovery, a large deposit of unique invertebrate fossils in the Burgess Shale on Mount Wapta. The Vaux family frequently visited his camp. After her marriage Mary moved to Washington where she remained until her death.

A vigorous and active woman, Mary was a member of a number of organizations: the Canadian and American Alpine Clubs, the American Association for the Advancement of Science, the Academy of Natural Sciences, the Association of Women Geographers (as national president) and the Photographic Society of Philadelphia. She succeeded George on the Board of Indian Commissioners in 1927 and served two terms, devoting a considerable amount of time travelling to inspect reservations. She was a major benefactor and guiding force in the building of the Florida Avenue Friends Meeting House after the election of President Herbert Hoover in 1928, the need being perceived for a suitable place of worship for a Quaker president.

A skilled botanical painter, Mary's flower drawings were published in 1925 by the Smithsonian Institution. *North American Wildflowers*, a limited edition, five volume set was referred to as "an Audubon of Botany." Ten years later another volume, *Illustrations of North American Pitcher Plants* was published. At age 65 Mary wrote in the foreword to *North American Wildflowers*:

Wild Flowers were a joy and inspiration in the happy days of childhood when I was taught to observe and sketch them under the direction of a skilled artist. Years passed before a botanical friend at Glacier, British Columbia, asked me to portray a rare and perishable alpine flower so as to preserve its beauty, color, and graceful outline as a living thing. During succeeding seasons I painted other rare specimens until many of the "living flowers that skirt in the eternal frost" in the wildflower gardens of the Canadian Rockies were transferred in color and form to the East . . . . I have spent from three to four months each season in the Canadian Rockies, where Dr. Walcott was carrying on geological explorations, covering in all more than five thousand miles on the mountain trails.

Mary M. Vaux and guide Robert Campbell, Lake O'Hara camp, 1907.

The Glacier Study

Of all the phenomena that attract the nature lover in the high mountains, possibly none is more interesting than the glaciers.

These vast bodies of ice, slowly meandering from the highest peaks and snow-submerged valleys, . . . ever pushing onward with resistless force, give us a picture of the operation and unchangeableness of natural laws, which is most impressive.

[George Vaux Jr., and William S. Vaux Jr. *Glacier Observations*, 1907]

In *Modern Glaciers*, William Vaux's last and most important monograph, he states that: "During railway construction the [Illecillewaet] glacier was doubtless often visited by those stationed on the work, but no records were made until July 17, 1887 when our party, passing through, roughly mapped the tongue and made a photographic record of the conditions as they existed." This realization of being first, and a fascination for the great ice beasts (with head walls, snouts, tongues, toes, and movement, glaciers are truly anthropomorphized) involved William in a study that lasted a life time. Twenty years of observation, and ten years of annual study and documentation, resulted in eight monographs on glaciers co-authored with his brother and several under his name alone. The study started, by circumstance, at the point of maximum glacial advance in the modern age and has remained as a record that is still consulted today while the Great Glacier has virtually disappeared.

The Vaux family initiated the first continuous, detailed glacier study in Canada. Though amateurs, their work was recognized by the Commission International des Glaciers, who reproduced one of William's monographs, the first time it recognized a non-commissioned study. After William's death George was appointed one of four commissioners of this body in the United States. Their data were used by a number of authors and scientists writing on the mountains of Canada. Dr. William Sherzer used their information and measuring points on the Illecillewaet to complete his study for the Smithsonian Institution, *Glaciers of the Canadian Rockies and Selkirks*, published in 1907. A number of their glacier photographs were used to illustrate publications on the mountains.

The Vauxes' claim that they were the first to photograph the Illecillewaet was accurate as far as they could determine at the time. O.B. Buell, an American photographer supported by the CPR, had photographed the Great Glacier in 1885 but these images had not been used publicly and remained unknown. The Vauxes were the first to recognize the importance of their very early photographs as a starting point for a study and the potential of the medium in recording the glaciers of Canada. A few casual surveys had been started between 1887 and 1897 when the Vauxes began their detailed work. These earlier studies were noted and, when possible, used by the family; but being of short duration and not properly documented, the observations were not very valuable.

As a Dominion Surveyor working in the Selkirks, and a founder of the Alpine Club of Canada, Arthur Oliver Wheeler was in a position to appreciate the work of the Vaux family. He was to assist the Vauxes a great deal over the years, and was in turn influenced by them. With the Alpine Club he took over the measuring of the Wapta (Yoho) Glacier that the Vauxes had begun in 1901. In 1898 he noted with approval that the Vauxes' survey of both the Illecillewaet and Asulkan Glaciers had become "properly systemized" and that William's extremely practical action of marking the magnetic variation on a window sill at Glacier House for all to see was "to be commended." (William corrected the official CPR map compass declination by 15 minutes.)

William S. Vaux Jr. taking a prismatic compass bearing.

That year, prismatic compass bearings were registered for a number of prominent points on the glaciers and surrounding landmarks; barometric readings to determine altitudes were taken whenever possible, sketch maps of the glaciers and detailed notes were made. For the first time they used a full plate (6½" x 8½" negative) view camera as well as their standard 4" x 5" camera to photograph the glaciers and surrounding area. They established standard photographic points and procedures to be used repeatedly as they made detailed, accurate measurements and photographs in eleven of the following fourteen years. Since photographing the glacier in 1887 had led to the inception of the glacial study, it was logical that photography would continue to be used extensively in their work. In retrospect these photographs remain as the single most important aspect of the study. The repeated views taken from the same point over a long period using the same equipment have resulted in a record of inestimable value.

They made the most detailed studies on the Illecillewaet and Asulkan Glaciers and over the years made less extensive but still significant observations on the Yoho, Victoria and Wenkchemna Glaciers. They also occasionally visited and photographed a number of other glaciers in the Canadian Rockies.

William was aware of the conflicting theories then prevalent concerning the flowing motion of glaciers which "involves a most difficult problem in ice physics which is not yet thoroughly solved. No fewer than nine theories have been advanced to explain the phenomena." He preferred to stay in the realm of observation, leaving the more obscure problems of the causes for others to delve into.

The Vauxes considered their role to be:

a) In mapping the end of the glacier, with its several moraines and surroundings, showing their conditions through a number of years
b) taking a series of "test photographs" in successive years from the same position
c) measuring the amount of recession from year to year
d) measuring the rate of flow.

To carry out the last two aims, they placed a row of specially made steel plates across the glacier, which they sighted from a fixed point along a base line. The position of each plate, measured over a period of time, indicated the overall rate of flow as well as the different flow rates for each part of the glacier. Sightings were also made on the plates to measure the amount of surface melt.

Plates were first placed in 1899, and replaced in 1906 and 1909 as the movement of the glacier caused them to disappear. The measurements were assisted by Mr. Duschesnay and other CPR employees who supplied equipment for the early surveys and made measurements at times when the Vauxes weren't in the mountains. The family eventually brought their own transit and equipment, and the CPR continued to support their activities through free guide service (to assist on the ice) and free rail passes. In return the Vauxes wrote and illustrated with their photographs a twenty page pamphlet, *The Glaciers of the Canadian Rockies & Selkirks* as a general introduction and explanation of the glacial phenomena. This publication was used as a promotional item by the railway from 1900 to well into the 'twenties, being updated by various family members as required.

After William's death, George and Mary required more outside assistance to make the measurements, and A. O. Wheeler, in particular, helped. George didn't return to the mountains after 1911, and Mary attempted to keep the study going. Her marriage and other interests caused her work to lapse after 1913, but she did update the CPR pamphlet as late as 1922. The survey that they had started on the Yoho Glacier was carried on for many years by A.O. Wheeler and the scientific section of the Alpine Club of Canada.

GLACIERS

AT THE LAKES IN THE CLOUDS, CANADIAN ROCKIES.

BY

GEORGE and WILLIAM S. VAUX, JR.

OF PHILADELPHIA, PENNA.

First edition of *Glaciers*, 1900.

The Photographs

George, William and Mary Vaux had been involved in photography since the early 1880s, and they were sophisticated in its use by the time they made their first pictures of the Great Glacier. The early recognition that their simple "snapshots" were of great importance in determining the movement of the glacier immediately suggested the extensive use of photography as a documentary measuring tool. Their images, activities and involvement in the photographic community, however, indicate that they considered photography as more than only a recording medium.

The Vauxes always considered themselves to be amateurs, without the pressures or pretensions of the professional or "high art" photographers. They were, however, involved in a medium invented, advanced and dominated by amateurs. Philadelphia was a major photographic centre in America, fostered by the Philadelphia Photographic Society, one of the oldest and most respected photographic organizations in the United States. Local manufacturers like John Carbutt, who introduced the first dry plate in the U.S. in 1879 and the first flexible sheet film in 1888, placed the Philadelphians on the leading edge of photographic advancement.

The invention of dry plate and flexible negative material in the early 1880s, delivered photography into the hands of the general public. The photographer still required great patience and skill but was finally freed from the exceptionally cumbersome wet plate process which had necessitated transporting a darkroom tent to sensitize and develop the negative. Smaller cameras and, eventually, the introduction of the Kodak (which basically started the photo-finishing business) in the late '80s brought photography to fad proportions by the turn of the century.

In 1884 George and Mary were members of a group of Philadelphians dedicated to the advancement of photography as an art form. William, then age twelve, was experimenting with simple pinhole cameras. The family's first trip west in 1885 had a distinct photographic overtone; young William illustrated a homemade book of the journey with photographs, and both George and Mary exhibited well-received landscape views of the Yellowstone area in an 1886 exhibition sponsored by the Photographic Society of Philadelphia.

The Photographic Society had a diverse membership including scientists, amateur and professional photographers. The *Journal* of the Society records that the membership received presentations on the most sophisticated level, from the pre-eminent work of Hurter and Driffield in photographic sensitometry through detailed explanations of his latest advances given by Philadelphian Frederick Ives, one of the earliest experimenters in colour photography. George and William held a number of positions on the executive of the Society over the years and participated on many committees. When the Society finally permitted women members in 1895, Mary and her friend, Mary Schäffer were among the first.

All three of the siblings gave presentations at the Society's meetings and participated in its exhibitions. William's talks were mainly on more technical matters such as standardization of materials and use of various techniques. Presentations of lantern slides and prints of their mountain photographs were given periodically, usually with George as spokesman. On one occasion he gave a few details on their technique, as recorded in the Society's *Journal*:

George Vaux, Jr. made a brief verbal communication upon the subject of "Mountain Photography," explaining the apparatus and processes employed in the work which he had done, in conjunction with his brother and sister, in British Columbia. He said that he used Cramer iso-chromatic plates and a color screen—preferably the Bausch & Lomb bichromate rayfilter. Exceedingly short exposures were necessary, even with the use of color screens. The striking cloud effects in most of the photographs

Mary and George Vaux Jr. on Mount Fairview, Lake Louise, August 24, 1904.

on the wall were due to some extent to the use of color screen and color-corrected plate, but not entirely so, for it was an unusual day in the Canadian Rockies when beautiful cloud negatives could not be secured. Mr. Vaux said that for distant views he had found the telephoto lens too heavy for the ordinary camera equipment, and that in his opinion the use of the back combination [convertible lens] was usually in every way more satisfactory. He described the method employed in making the panoramas shown, the camera being carefully leveled and pivoted, the chief trouble, of course, being the accurate matching of the negatives.

Mary gave some more information on the use of photography in the mountains, in an article she wrote for the *Canadian Alpine Journal*:

A kodak, if no larger instrument can be managed, yields most satisfactory results, although the better records from a larger sized camera are an increased delight, when one has the patience and skill to obtain them. For changing plates in camp, an improvised tepee can be made of the blankets, and, if this is done after sundown, is quite satisfactory. We have never known plates to be fogged by the operation. Cut films are more convenient than glass plates, as they are so much lighter and not subject to breakage, although not so easily handled. The actinic properties of the light are very great and care must be used to avoid overexposure.

The Vauxes, as part of the Photographic Society and through their friendship with Robert S. Redfield and John Bullock, two local leaders in the "photography as art" movement, were interested in more than the technical aspects of photography and took an active part in the furtherance of the medium as an art form. The Society had held salons in conjunction with the New York and Boston societies since 1887. In a dramatic break with tradition, the Philadelphians, under the influence of Alfred Stieglitz, and with George Vaux Jr. as chairman of the salon committee, embarked on a new tack:

The Philadelphia Photographic Salon of 1898 was the first photographic exhibition held in America confined exclusively to pictures selected by a jury for their high artistic merit, with no awards other than the honor of acceptance. The plan involved such a long step in advance that of necessity it was largely experimental. Your committee, however, were strong in the belief that artistic photography in America had advanced to a stage justifying and demanding such an exhibition.

The traditional salon style was to hang every submission and give a multitude of awards in a vast number of categories. The new, more rigid approach was intended to raise the standards of photography as an art form, as was being done in Europe by groups like England's "Linked Ring."

As committee chairman George Vaux was responsible for gaining the support of Alfred Stieglitz for the 1899 exhibition. Stieglitz was reticent, not being overly impressed with the abilities of the committee (including George). He did lend his support, however, and suggested the involvement of people like F. Holland Day, Gertrude Kasebier and Clarence H. White on the jury. Stieglitz himself served on the jury for the contentious 1900 salon. A growing backlash had developed against the "Fine Art" group's showing "the product of one narrow, limited, rather egotistical school." In the 1901 executive election, George Vaux ran for president of the Society as representative of the progressive group. He lost, precipitating the resignation of all the supporters of the art movement from the Society.

In February of 1902, Stieglitz formed his now famous Photo-Secession out of frustration with the established photographic groups. Both George and Mary were associate members. In the "Little Galleries of the Photo-Secession at 291 Fifth Avenue, New York" or simply called "291", Alfred Stieglitz firmly established the New American School in photography, then went on to become an important influence in contemporary art in America by being the first to exhibit European painters like Matisse, Cezanne and Picasso in his gallery.

EXHIBITION OF PHOTOGRAPHS. THE WORK OF MARY M. VAUX, GEORGE VAUX, JR., WILLIAM S. VAUX, JR.

AT THE PHOTOGRAPHIC SOCIETY OF PHILADELPHIA, 10 SOUTH EIGHTEENTH ST., FROM MARCH SIXTH TO THIRTIETH, 10 A.M., TO 5 P.M., DAILY EXCEPT SUNDAYS

MDCCCCI

Exhibition catalogue cover.

It's doubtful whether the "photography as art" argument will ever be resolved. At that time the two main camps were the "pictorialists," who believed in the manipulation of the print or negative in search of artistic expression; and the "straight" photographers who advocated the integrity of the medium and who abhorred artifice. Both groups supported the medium as a means of artistic expression through the rendering of subtleties of light. The battle still continues, the combatants having altered the dialogue but little.

Many photographers, including the Vauxes, stayed out of the fray and settled on a happy compromise. Using all the standard pictorial presentation conventions in the elegant style of the European salons, they mounted their prints on complementary dark-coloured paper, in large frames, signed with a simple, designed monogram. They used matt platinum paper to maximize tonal rendition and moderate the amount of detail by slightly softening the image. They were still "straight" photographs however.

Though totally immersed in the politics and organization of the important Philadelphia salons, George and Mary didn't exhibit in them. Mary did show some photographs in two Secession shows in 1904 and in the first members' exhibition at "291" in 1905. They appear to have been caught up in the excitement of the period which was perceived as the birth of an important movement. As did many early supporters of the Photo-Secession, the Vauxes allowed their interest to wane as Stieglitz concentrated more on abstract painting than photography. Their involvement in the fine art movement was minimal after the first few years.

William had little to do with the art movement and did not involve himself in the political battles, remaining on as treasurer of the Photographic Society after his sister and brother resigned. He made his attitude towards contemporary art quite clear in his diary:

I for one was almost willing to forgive some of the impressionists school and to accept their often fearful rendering of color as not so much a transgression of harmony. But colors when seen mixed by the hand of nature are as different from the daub of so called artists as is an old master to the work of the vainest tyro.

As Quakers, with a traditional reticence towards art, the family seems to have found a pleasant compromise in photography. The "art born of science" served them well as a tool in the glacier studies, it also gave them a creative outlet. Art for art's sake was alien to Quaker beliefs; as late as 1882 the official doctrine was that the "appreciation of art led to unholy thought." Art as illustration, however, was of high merit. The liberalizing of the Quaker Discipline, or "the curing of the Puritan hangover" towards the end of the 19th century, allowed the Vauxes to be members of a totally revolutionary art movement. Their traditions always kept them on the periphery.

With George's and Mary's interest in photographing the mountain landscape and William's increasing involvement in the glacial studies, their photographic productivity and skill increased steadily into the twentieth century. The two brothers did most of the actual taking of the pictures in the mountains, particularly with the large cameras, but Mary's involvement in that aspect grew steadily and increased dramatically after William's death. Mary was responsible for the technical work on the photographs and did all of the printing. She made platinum prints exclusively, having learned the process from William Rau, a local professional photographer and a master printer. The prints were made on a German paper using a hot development technique. Her skill as a painter was utilized in hand colouring lantern slides, a practice which evolved into good natured but heated competition with Mary Schäffer.

The mountain work was exhibited collectively and stood as a common front. They sought neither acclaim nor reward but presented their photographs to the world as renderings of a landscape integral to their lives. Unfortunately their mountain photographs were not very well received by the pictorialist community of the day. In a review of one exhibit the writer states: "the work of Messrs. George and William Vaux Jr., does not aim at a very high pictorial standard, but is always interesting . . . ." The same writer waxes poetic about a number of pictures, by others, with titles like "In the Fold," "Child with Book," and "Two Little Brothers," and refers to Mary's photograph called "Sheep Pasture" as "a very pleasing little thing, simple and unaffected and very well arranged." It's not surprising that the unfamiliar mountain views were not met with approval.

The Vaux family was exceptional in the technical and aesthetic mastery of photographing the impossibly hard-edged northern mountain light that cuts and shatters a scene rather than modelling it. Establishing foreground or attaining good vantage points in the mountains of Canada requires a great deal of effort and patience. The Vauxes, through dedication and persistence, produced a significant body of work that places them among the select few who have captured a portion of the mountain essence.

Viewed today, the photographs are enhanced with the patina of nostalgia. Antiquated steam engines and buildings take the viewer back to a period when everything was new. Images of people, long dead, in quaint old-fashioned clothing give us a rosy sense of human continuity. The era depicted is without today's feelings of environmental guilt. People were considered as an integral aspect of the wilderness, not interlopers. The photographs made by the Vaux family are the reflection and record of the Victorian attitude that the vast defile was to be translated into human terms for the benefit of man. Their photographic skill, artistry and depth of understanding of the mountain environment have created a powerful and incisive document of a living wilderness.

The role of man in the environment has changed. The mountain wilderness the Vaux family experienced has been altered through natural forces and the hand of man. The great cataracts of ice have subsided into the stillness of the névé. The Vauxes left us a legacy of images frozen in time.

FOLIO

A glimpse of Mount Victoria, Lake Louise, July 25, 1900.

Falls in the ice of the Great Glacier, July 4, 1894.
The glacier feature depicted, caused by surface meltwater eroding the ice, is called a moulin or mill hole.

Test picture of the Illecillewaet Glacier, 1902.

Dome, Castor and Pollux, Asulkan Glacier, Glacier Crest, and Illecillewaet Glacier from trail to Mount Avalanche, 1898.

Ice forefoot of Illecillewaet Glacier, August 17, 1899.
Mary Vaux with ice axe.

Castor, Pollux etc. with Asulkan stream in foreground, Aug. 26, 1898.

Asulkan Pass and Glacier and Mounts Fox, Deville, Dawson, Castor, Pollux from bench on Mount Abbott trail, July 26, 1897.

Mount Stephen and Kicking Horse Bridge, July 30, 1901.

Bridge construction, July 14, 1900.
Glacier House area.

Break in snowshed at Glacier from below, Glacier Crest in distance, 1898.
The workmen are repairing a snowshed crushed by an avalanche. The "summer track" which allows a better view passes on the right.

Engine No. 738 at Field, July 3, 1900.
The engineer, Lew Patrick, got the polished brass flagstaff for his engine from the Vauxes.

CPR Hotel from Tunnel Mountain, Banff, June 21, 1900.

Christian Häsler and Edouard Feuz, Guides, Glacier House, Aug. 16, 1899.

Camp at Lake Marion, July 28, 1897.

Woods, trail to Cascades, showing large cedar trees, August 27, 1898.

Glacier Table, Lake Louise, July 29, 1900.
George Vaux Jr. standing on a rock which has retarded the melting of its supporting ice.

Yoho Glacier, 1906.

Asulkan Glacier, 1905.

Victoria Glacier, July 7, 1900.
William Vaux Jr., Hemreich (guide), George Vaux, Georgena Cresson, Caleb Cresson, Christian Häsler (guide).

Mount Dawson and Dawson Glacier from Asulkan Pass, July 14, 1901.
Mary Vaux with guides.

Crevasses, Illecillewaet Glacier, 1905.

Large serac and group, Illecillewaet Glacier, June 29, 1900.

Looking north from Abbot Pass, 1902.
Mount Victoria and the Victoria Glacier.

Summit of Mount Stephen, July 21, 1900.

Emerald Range and North Boulder Valley from Boulder Creek Bridge, July 18, 1900.
The peaks are part of what we now call the President Range, near Field, B.C.

Mount Assiniboine from camp, 1907.

Takakkaw Falls from below, August 19, 1901.

Mount Niles and Mount Daly from Upper Yoho Valley, 1906.
The Upper Yoho is now called the Little Yoho Valley.

Mount Cathedral from Lake O'Hara, 1902.

Pope's Peak and Mount Victoria from railroad above Hector Station, August 13, 1901.
Sink Lake is in the foreground.

Mount Temple in cloud from near Ptarmigan Lake, 1906.

Right hand half of panorama of moraine of Illecillewaet Glacier from Rock E., August 11, 1899.
Rock E. is one of the many standard points established by the Vaux family to measure glacial movements.

GLACIER HOUSE SCRAPBOOK

Glacier House was one of the first of Canada's mountain hotels. Its wilderness location and the imposing mountain peaks of the Selkirk Range made it a popular tourist destination and the first centre for North American alpinism. The *Scrapbook*, a register/comment book kept for the hotel visitors, is a unique record of the Victorian involvement in the "Canadian Alps."

The popularity of the mountain region was an added bonus for the Canadian Pacific Railway. The mountains had initially been considered mainly as insurmountable barriers to the ports of British Columbia. The route through them was chosen out of political and economic expediency rather than any master plan to feature the alpine landscape. The first mountain hostels were built to save the considerable expense of hauling heavy dining cars over the excessively steep grades of the hastily constructed line rather than as destinations in themselves.

To run the rail line through Rogers Pass in the Selkirk Range, the engineers added an extra four miles of track looped in a figure eight to lower the grade and avoid the worst of the avalanche slopes. The "Loops," the miles of snowsheds that protected the rails from the frequent avalanches, and bridges like Stoney Creek (claimed to be the highest railway bridge in the world) made the whole of Rogers Pass an engineering marvel of the day.

One of the loops brought the tracks within sight of the Great Glacier of the Illecillewaet (Indian for swift running water), an imposing cascade of ice surrounded by a stunning array of peaks. The dining car, temporarily parked near the foot of the glacier, was replaced in January of 1887 with a station building and dining room with six guest rooms. Seven hundred and eight people stayed in the tiny hotel that year. Whether they came in search of a wilderness adventure or were in transit on the "Imperial Highway" to the Far East, few of the guests were unmoved by the power of the mountain landscape. Many of the early visitors, like the Vaux family, were profoundly affected by the mountains; seduced by the virgin wilderness, they would return year after year, adopting the area as their spiritual home.

The CPR, quick to realize the tourist potential of the mountains, embarked on extensive promotion campaigns, coining the term "Canadian Alps" to unite the distinct Rocky and Selkirk mountain ranges. Like Glacier House, the other dining facilities, Mount Stephen House at Field and Fraser Canyon House at North Bend, became small hotels. The railway built larger, more elegant hotels at Banff and Lake Louise, promoting tourism through a strange combination of luxury and wilderness, directing its advertising at the wealthy and well-educated. Attracted to the Canadian west by the romance of wilderness adventure and the sense of discovery in a new land, the Victorian traveller still expected the comforts of modern society.

Much to the disdain of the Glacier House regulars, Banff and Lake Louise quickly grew into tourist meccas with the attendant hawkers of cheap tourist paraphernalia and "civilized" distractions. In contrast, because of its rugged setting and very short (mid-July to early-September) season, Glacier House remained a wilderness hotel and attracted a clientele dedicated to the active, outdoor enjoyment of the mountains. Though the CPR may have been aware of the potential of Glacier as an alpine centre, it wasn't until 1899 that the company finally listened to the repeated suggestions that Swiss guides be hired to facilitate climbing in the area.

Alpinism was a relatively new sport, which developed, primarily under British influence, in the 1850s. By the 1880s all the major peaks of Europe had been scaled and alpinists turned their attention to the newly accessible Canadian mountains. The first experienced climbers to visit Glacier were the Reverend William Spotswood Green and Henry Swanzy in 1888; they were soon followed by other British climbers like H.E.M. Stutfield, J. Norman Collie and members of various European alpine clubs. The first ascents of the largest peaks surrounding Glacier had been

Train on the Loop, July 29, 1897.

MAP OF
GLACIER
PARK
GLACIER PARK
Scale: 3 miles to an inch
Photo-zincographed at the Surveyor-General's office, Ottawa, Canada.

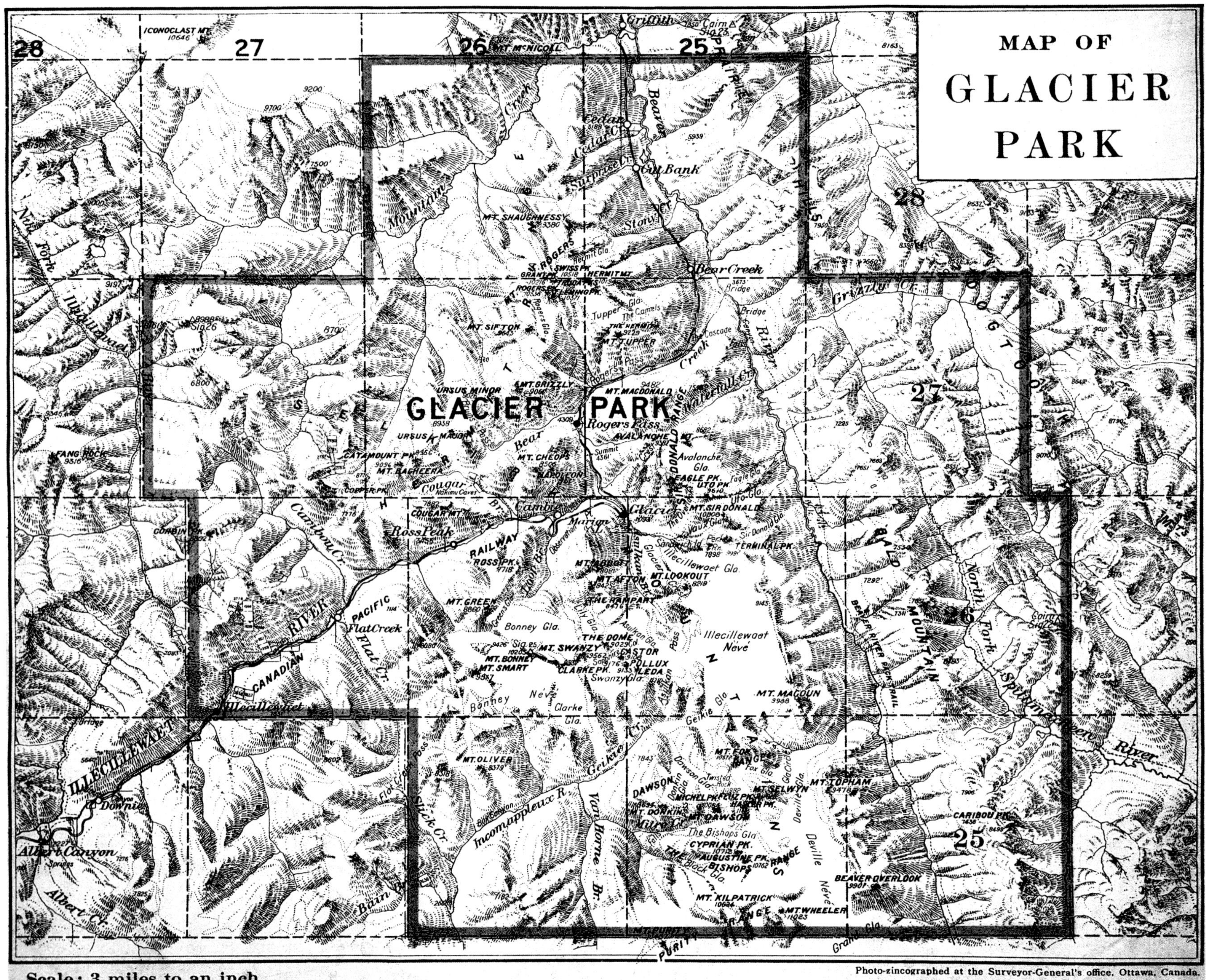

ca 1910.

achieved by the time the guides arrived, but there were many untouched mountains and new routes to establish. The introduction of the Swiss guides allowed both the amateur climber and the tourist to travel much more extensively in the mountains. The "golden age" of Glacier had begun and the sport of alpinism was firmly established in North America.

Dr. J.H. Stallard, a frequent guest at Glacier House, started the *Scrapbook*. He had made repeated appeals to the CPR to establish a minute book, in which visitors could record their impressions. He argued that those who arrived during one of the all too common rainy days in the Selkirks would have no reason to stay, being unaware of the scenic splendour, many attractions and activities at Glacier House. The company was eventually convinced and the book was started in 1897. By filling the first eleven pages of the ledger sized book with his effusive praise of the scenery and detailed accounts of trips in the area, Dr. Stallard set the style and standard for the entries that followed. The effect of the Selkirks on the Victorian traveller was not subtle; the "majestic, magnificent, lordly mountains" and the "luxuriant, forest primeval" stirred the souls of many. Visitors were repeatedly reminded of the "insignificance of humanity, in the presence of the mighty forces of nature...."

Members of the Vaux family were among the most regular contributors to the *Scrapbook*. Their handwritten entries were augmented over the years by copies of their various monographs and booklets, which were replaced repeatedly as they were stolen until finally going out of print. The Vauxes' "scientific notebook" for Glacier House, which was reserved for more empirical observations, has not survived.

The Chalet at Lake Louise had a similar record book, and since the same group of people visited all the hotels, there was quite likely one for Mount Stephen House at Field. The Glacier House *Scrapbook* is the only account of its kind to have survived.

The period covered by the book, 1897-1910, was truly a "golden age." The hotel grew to have ninety rooms and all the conveniences of the day, including a bowling alley. The number of Swiss guides steadily increased and they were always in demand. Glacier had become the centre of North American alpinism. By 1910 mountaineers had made all of the first ascents in the area and were going further afield, only occasionally using Glacier House as a base. The hotel still had its loyal following and tourist climbers, but the sense of discovery was gone.

In 1916 the Connaught Tunnel was completed under Mount Macdonald. The five mile, double track tunnel lowered the grade through the Selkirks, and eliminated the use of Rogers Pass and the "Loops." Glacier House was no longer required as a dining service for the passengers. Instead of the once famous view of the "heart of the Selkirks" all that the railway passengers saw was the blackness of the tunnel. Since the train no longer stopped in front of the hotel, the number of guests steadily declined. The fear of fire after the burning of the Chalet at Lake Louise in 1924 caused the company to close the wood frame Glacier House in 1925, and it was torn down in 1929. A planned two-hundred room stone structure was never built.

The *Scrapbook* was the work of many people of varying levels of involvement, literacy and legibility (contrary to popular myth, not everyone in the nineteenth century had excellent penmanship). The old volume had been roughly treated before being copied and lost. Difficulties in transcription notwithstanding, the volume was edited to one third of its original length for this publication due to its size and the excess of redundant material. Such editing imparts some bias; however, every effort has been made to maintain the tone and balance of the original. The more literate and humorous entries have won out over the redundant, dry, silly, or irrelevant contributions of both the day visitor and the serious alpinists. The earlier entries, with their evocation of discovery and awe, have taken precedence over the latter. In some years entries were few in number, and this edited version maintains that sense of proportion.

To ease reading and facilitate understanding, spellings have been standardized and some of the grammar modified. The scrawl and patina of the original are gone, but the words remain as an intriguing reflection of the Victorian experience in the "Canadian Alps."

Glacier House, August, 1897.

**All the photographs in this version of the* Scrapbook, *except for the few otherwise credited, are by the Vaux family.*

Panorama view from Mt. Abbot
Photo by J. Howard A. Chapman, Victoria B. C.
Catamount Peak 8956
Ursus Major 8933
Mt. Cheops 8506
Mt. Napoleon 7737
Mt. Grizzly
Mt. Sifton 9643
Rogers Pass Summit 4361
Mt. Hermit 10194
Mt. Tupper 9227
The Camels
Mt. McDonald 9484
Mt. Avalanche 9387
Eagle Peak 9353
Uto Peak 9610
Mt. Sir Donald 10808
Terminal Pk. 9773
Perley Rock 7873
Illecillewaet Glacier
Illecillewaet Névé
Mt. Lookout 8219
Mt. Macoun
Asulkan Valley
Asulkan Glacier
Mt. Fox 10048
Mt. Dawson 11110
Asulkan Pass 7710

ca 1900.

THIS SCRAPBOOK IS ESTABLISHED IN ORDER THAT THE VISITORS TO GLACIER HOUSE SHOULD HAVE THE OPPORTUNITY TO ENTER THEIR EXPERIENCES OF AND OPINIONS ON, THE SCENERY WITHIN THEIR REACH; AND THUS TO ENCOURAGE OTHERS TO ENJOY THE SUPERB VIEWS TOO OFTEN PASSED BY TRAVELLERS IN IGNORANCE OF THEIR EXISTENCE AND OF THEIR ACCESSIBILITY TO ORDINARY TOURISTS. VISITORS ARE THEREFORE RESPECTFULLY REQUESTED TO REGISTER THEIR NAMES AND ADDRESSES; TOGETHER WITH ANY SUCH OBSERVATIONS AND REMARKS AS THEY MAY DESIRE TO MAKE.

Sept. 8, 1897 Dr. J. H. Stallard* and Mrs. Stallard—Menlo Park, San Mateo County, Cal. have now completed their fourth visit to Glacier House and it may not be uninteresting to casual visitors detained by bad weather or the glorious mountain scenery to relate those varied experiences on an early page of this scrapbook.

We left San Francisco on the 18th of July 1896 and after an uneventful voyage arrived in Victoria & proceeded to Vancouver only to find the entire country enveloped in dense smoke. The road to Nanaimo was impassable. The whole region was alive with forest fires, largely caused by a swarm of mine prospectors then invading British Columbia. Thinking to escape this scourge we took the train to Glacier House. On the way nothing five hundred yards away was visible. We saw nothing of mountains; all was obscured, and when we arrived at Glacier House, the great Glacier was invisible & the cascade opposite the hotel was barely visible. We left the next day. Our first visit was a most lamentable failure.

On the 13th of August we returned to Glacier. Rain had in the meantime fallen, the fires were extinguished & the smoke had disappeared and we at once recognized that the modest railroad hotel forms the centre of a mountain region which rivals the Alps of Switzerland in beauty, sublimity and grandeur.

From the veranda of the hotel we see to the north the Hermit Range of mountains with Hermit towards the eastern extremity, Swiss Peaks in the foreground, & the pyramid of Cheops on the west, each with its attendant glacier, its snow clad summit, and its verdant base. In the valley at the foot the rushing Illecillewaet a thousand feet below. In this view is illustrated the special peculiarity of the Selkirk Mountains when compared with ranges of mountains further south. Here the peaks are bold, ragged & bare, but yet flecked with snow to the very summit. They look higher than they really are. There the snow lies low down upon their sides and decorates all their couloirs and ravines, and the timber line fights with the snow & the glaciers for the possession of the meeting line—and the forest at the base is but a rich foil which sets off the beauty of the snow flecked peaks & the light and glowing clouds above them. To the south the view is similar in principle but on more gigantic scale. On the southeast is Mt. Sir Donald, the Matterhorn of the Selkirks—a pyramid of solid rock which has only been ascended twice. It is flanked on the West by the Great Illecillewaet Glacier which falls in broken masses for several thousand feet. The Glacier is bounded on the west by a ridge called Glacier Crest, the summit of which is said to give a fine view of the Asulkan Glacier which descends from the Asulkan Pass, but as yet the trail is not practicable for ladies.

**Joshua Harrison Stallard (1821–1899), a noted English physician teaching at the medical school of the University of California, was an experienced alpinist who climbed in the Alps as early as 1852. After his first visit to Glacier House in 1891, he wrote to the CPR's passenger traffic manager David McNicoll that visitor books "in which the travellers may record their experiences, their impressions of the scenery, their excursions . . . etc." would be of great advantage in the mountain hotels. He also suggested the company hire Swiss guides. By 1897 his suggestions were beginning to be incorporated.*

Asulkan Pass Early in the nineties a trail had been opened up the valley & a sign post had been erected to indicate its commencement. A hut had also been built in the Fish Valley on the southern side of the pass. But few persons had ever passed over & both hut & trail had disappeared leaving nothing but the sign post. In company with Mr. Perley* the proprietor of the hotel & the gardener as guide, we started soon after 5 o'clock A.M. There had been a thunderstorm the night before, but the air was now fresh & clear. After one mile of open trail we crossed the glacier stream and entered a thick undergrowth of alder. Every trace of the trail had disappeared & for two hours we scrambled through the dripping foliage. In less than five minutes we were all wet through to the shoulders and when we emerged from the forest some pints of water were wrung out of Mrs. Stallard's skirts. No one happily takes any harm from such exposures in the mountains, and after an hour's climbing over the rough stony moraine we became warm and comfortable. And now a new trouble presented itself. It was necessary to cross the stream and the bridge had been swept away so that we had to wade over our boots in ice cold water. This done we climbed up to a steep bank of slippery grass, the only denizen of which was a huge porcupine quite as anxious to escape from us as we from him. On reaching the margin of the glacier we took a little rest and refreshment in full enjoyment of the fresh air & brilliant sunshine. The view of Mt. Macdonald on the south of Rogers Pass is here particularly fine. We were now tied all together with a long rope in order to save any who might by possibility fall into a crevasse hidden by the snow which had fallen during the storm of the night before. This snow was soft and made our progress difficult; nevertheless we worked our way upwards until stopped by a huge crevasse. It was deep and its clear blue walls overhung the chasm. We skirted the edge towards the west & coming round the end resumed the ascent to the divide now plainly seen in front of us. It was noon when we arrived at the summit both tired and hungry. We set out our luncheon on a knoll of rocks near by & quaffed our champagne to the health of the first white lady who had climbed to this lovely spot to enjoy one of the most superb mountain views in the world. Not a cloud seen. . . . After a most delightful sojourn we started on our way home. The course was now easy. We almost ran down the soft snow slopes. On arriving at the glacier stream we found it much augmented by the melting of the snow under the warm sunshine, & some courage was required to cross it; but necessity has no law and we faced the unpleasant task. On reaching the timber belt we were greeted by millions of mosquitoes. The largest and most voracious we had ever seen. We completely lost the trail and fighting our way through the undergrowth we at length rushed through the open trail and arrived at Glacier House in time for supper and in the happy prospect of a refreshing bath and comfortable bed. I must not forget to note that "Sport" the hotel dog was our faithful attendant all the way. He paid every one in turn a visit of inquiry into his health & safety and I venture to think not only that he enjoyed the expedition quite as much as the next, but that he felt the same fatigue. Next morning he remained in bed & was aroused at noon with difficulty.

Harry A. Perley (1849-1933) was a former chief steward on the Allan Steamship Lines who had managed a restaurant for the CPR in Manitoba. In 1887 he contracted to manage Glacier House in return for the receipts from the hotel and dining room. He held the contract until it was terminated by the CPR in 1897. From 1889 to 1904 he owned the Alberta Hotel in Calgary.

Edward J. Duschesnay, Dr. J. H. Stallard, and George Vaux Jr. on a speeder, Glacier, August 1, 1897.

July 15th, 1897 Arrived at Glacier. Weather unsettled and the rainfall for the season unusually large.

July 16 Break of sunshine, only short walks possible.

July 17 Inspected the Asulkan Trail with M. Duchesnay,* found it impassable.

July 18 Went to Marion Lake. Ordered a trail to be cut to Observation Point & settled the site of a tent for the accommodation of tourists wishing to ascend Mount Abbott.

Edward J. Duschesnay was assistant-general superintendent of the Pacific Division of the CPR, headquartered at Revelstoke. In September, 1901, a rock fell on his head while he was directing the repair of a tunnel near Spuzzum, B.C. and killed him.

July 19 Weather unsettled.

July 20 do. do.

July 21 do. do.

July 22 do. do.

July 23 do. do.

July 24 do. do.

July 25 In the afternoon the weather began to improve; one by one the peaks became clear of cloud and a party was formed to spend the night in the tent erected at Marion Lake & to ascend Mt. Abbott next day. After supper accompanied by Mr. Geo. Vaux and Miss Vaux of Philadelphia we ascended to the tent & were received by Sam Youwell the guide. We found a rousing fire and second supper ready. All were entertained by stories & it was nearly midnight before we retired to roost.

July 26 We turned out at 4 am to find a cloudless sky and a rising barometer—some indications of a fine day. The breakfast was a chef-d'oeuvre—the tea & coffee excellent, the eggs & bacon delicious and the bannocks altogether worthy of an experienced Scotch prospector. We got away at 5:20. Our course lay first through the forest and then up a steep couloir of stones. We arrived on the first bench about 7 o'clock & sat down for a long rest & to admire the magnificent view.

Climbing the grassy slopes we came to a small lake & to a steep bluff reaching to the crest of the mountain. This we rounded on the north shoulder; we found a bed of snow which we crossed to a bench of huge rocks from which we saw the mountains of the west and their attendant glaciers, all now brilliant in the morning sun. Here we rested several hours, took luncheon & enjoyed a rest. At noon we arranged to signal our presence on the summit to Mr. Vaux Sr. on the snow sheds above Glacier House. This was successfully done by the use of mirror. Under the conduct of Sam Youwell we now passed along the brow of the mountain until we reached the highest peak, where we remained spellbound by the magnificence of the view.

Before descending we encountered a distinguished party of experienced mountaineers, accompanied by their guide from Zermatt, Switzerland. Nowhere in the world, said to me Professor Dixon* of Owens College Manchester England, is to be found a view more sublime or a day's journey more deeply interesting. We descended to the tent for tea and were met by many friends. We arrived at the Glacier House in good time for supper, our minds stored with remembrances which will only be effaced by death. July 27 was devoted to rest and the development of photographs. As most of my plates had been too much exposed I resolved to pay a second visit to Mt. Abbott in company with Mr. Wm. Vaux & Sam Youwell. We left the hotel after dinner and found the tent now equipped with new blankets much drier and more comfortable.

**Harold Bailey Dixon (1852-1932) was a British mountaineer who first visited the Canadian Rockies in 1897. His journey was inspired by the death of his friend Philip Abbot on Mount Lefroy the previous year. In an attempt to organize as strong a party as possible to complete the climb on which Abbot had died, Dixon brought his favourite guide from the Alps, Peter Sarbach of Saint Niklaus, Switzerland. Sarbach was the first professional European guide to climb in western Canada.*

July 28 We rose at 4:30 & got on the trail soon after five o'clock. On ascending we took a new & easier route to the bench & from the bench a more direct climb to the summit. We enjoyed a long rest; took many pictures & rounding the northern shoulder descended almost directly to the lake.

July 29 Arrangements were made for an excursion to the Asulkan pass. The party to consist of Dr. & Mrs. Stallard, Dr. Helena Goodwin, Messrs George & Wm. Vaux of Philadelphia, Professor Dixon of Owens College Manchester & his Zermatt guide Sarbach, Sam Youwell as chief guide and one porter.

July 30 We were aroused at 4 am & assembled for breakfast at 4:30. We left the hotel at 5:10 am. The trail through the forest had been well opened but the bridge across the glacier had not yet been erected. Instead of ascending by the grassy slope as last year we followed the crest of the moraine at the top of which we reached the snowfield. Here we stopped for breakfast & a rest. During the ascent from the forest there is a fine view of the icefall which is rapid & heavily crevassed. On the other side the Dome, the Castor & Pollux. The Rampart & Mt. Abbott are conspicuous & looking back is a fine view of Mt. Macdonald. All harnessed with double length of rope we embarked upon the snow field. The crevasses were threaded and the bridges roped and in less than an hour we were safe in the middle of the snow field with the col in sight. On arriving, pictures, rest & luncheon were the orders of the day & were fully enjoyed by all. Very soon however the peaks to the west & north began to be obscured by cloud & the wind began to blow over the divide. It began to lighten around Sir Donald & ere long we experienced the sublime effects of a thunder storm in the higher regions. We took temporary shelter from the snow & hailstones under the rocks on the western side of the pass. Soon the sky began to clear. We then resumed our ropes & went down the snow field in a warming trot. In descending Mrs. Stallard put her foot into a deep crevasse and her example was followed by Professor Dixon. Both recovered themselves without assistance, but such experience demonstrates the value of the rope. At the bottom of the moraine the sun shone out brightly & we rested to exhaust the contents of the refreshment sack. The march home through the dripping wet forest was fatiguing but we reached Glacier House before one o'clock. In the evening bad weather again set in & it rained in torrents.

J. H. Stallard, M. D., London
Menlo Park, San Mateo Co. California

Sam Youwell, Mrs. Stallard, Dr. Helena Goodwin, George Vaux Jr., unknown, Dr. J. H. Stallard, Harold B. Dixon, and Peter Sarbach on way to Asulkan Pass, July 30, 1897.

Thursday July 7th, 1898 In July of 1890 I came out to Donald. I there engaged as my companion the most celebrated bear-hunter of the region who had spent the first 14 years of his life as an Arab of the London streets. This early experience in the sharpening of his wits had evidently not unfitted him for wood-craft. In getting through intricate forests I have never seen his equal. He came with me to Rogers Pass station one afternoon whence we ascended to the top of the tree line and camped out in our sleeping bags.

The next morning we climbed the rounded dome-like snow slope which forms the n.e. extremity of the Hermit Ledge (which may be seen from the Glacier House).

No difficulties presented themselves except a few crevasses which we skirted. The views were very fine. We descended to the pass lying between our white summit and the massive rocky peak to the n.e., and thence to the Glacier House. The next day we arose early & ascended the valley to the left of Mt. Sir Donald, as one faces him, to the foot of the cliffs. At that point one discovers when he reaches the very cliffs, to the left of Sir Donald, that a stratum runs from the top of the cliff (or what may be termed the gum) down to the base of the cliff or gum at a very gentle angle. This stratum projects about 18 inches and forms an easy path of ascent to the north or left base of Sir Donald. We then ascended the tooth for about 800 feet. At this point my bear-hunter gave out and we were obliged of course to descend.

It is certain that the summit will never be reached by way of this ledge. Two days after it was reached from the other side (for the first time) by two members of the German or Swiss Alpine Club* assisted by my bear-hunter.

In July 1891 I came here again with the purpose of taking photos rather than making ascensions. Yesterday with my companions, Geo. F. Bentley of New York and Francis F. Adams of Milwaukee, I went to the top of Mt. Abbott from whence we enjoyed a magnificent view. Today we visited what may be termed the ledge of Eagle Peak at the head of Cascade Valley. I consider the view from this point somewhat superior to that from Mt. Abbott. We beheld the peaks rising throughout the whole circumference of the horizon except what may be hidden by the stupendous cliffs of Eagle Peak and Sir Donald, whose proximity adds impressiveness. I have had the privilege of spending summers in the various portions of the Alps but feel no disposition to make any invidious comparisons. This view (from Eagle Ledge) certainly superior to the one from Piz Langard in the Engadine. One feature of the valley which does not exist in a like degree among the Alps is the forests of great pines.

In 1891 I camped out for some time with a half-breed in the neighborhood of Lake Louise and am still entranced with the great beauty, picturesqueness and grandeur of its scenery. We expect to leave tomorrow for that locality visiting en route some of the peaks between Field and Laggan.

B. S. Comstock
New York City

The first ascent was made on July 26, 1890, by Emil Huber (1865-1939) and Carl Sulzer (1865-1934), both members of the Swiss Alpine Club. The "bear-hunter" was Harry Cooper. Benjamin Sayre Comstock (1859-1941) first climbed in the Alps as early as 1873. He was head of Comstock Manufacturing Co. and a director of 3-in-1 Oil Co. Comstock went on to climb Avalanche Mountain and attempted Rogers Peak. He remained actively involved in mountaineering in the Selkirks for many years.

July 7, 1898

Some advice may be of use to visitors who wish to attempt some climbing:

Try every stone, even the most solid looking boulder, before resting one of your feet upon it. They are apt to turn over at the slightest touch and then to form a trap for the humble ankle, withdrawing from which is, if possible, very painful.

Do not try to hasten your descent by sliding down the glacier ice in a sitting position—even the smallest distance done in that way would remind you lively of a hurdle race on the back of a porcupine, the ice being constituted by endless hard and sharp crystal needles.

[Anon]

Aug. 21, 1898

On the northeast platform opposite the dining room windows will be found two lines of tacks radiating from a common point. The left hand line represents the time meridian, and has an arrow mark and the letter "N" at the end. This line was obtained by observation. The right-hand line represents the magnetic meridian as it existed on August 13th, 1898, the variation being 24 degrees 45 minutes.

William S. Vaux, Jr.

Aug. 24, 1898

The traveller who again visits the great glacier of the Illecillewaet after a lapse of several years is almost sure to be struck with the fact that the mass of ice does not extend so far into the valley as it formerly did. Among the trees and alder bushes which cover the valley below the expanse of bare boulders may be found the remains of several terminal moraines, which give conclusive proof that the recession of the glacier was arrested at that point, only to continue again after the lapse of a short period.

In order that those who have never made glacial action a study may understand some of the rudimentary principles, it may not be out of place to roughly outline the way in which a glacier is formed, its gradual flow to the valley and its final disappearance at the stream which flows from beneath its foot.

The source of the glacier is in the great snow field or névé which covers the comparatively level portions of the higher mountain ranges. By the action of the sun and pressure this snow is very much compressed, till the crystals are frozen together and form clear ice. It is at this point that the glacier proper begins.

W. S. Vaux Jr. photographing the Illecillewaet Glacier from "Observation Rock," August, 1898.

Whilst ice cannot be made to flow like water as we consider it in the ordinary sense, yet when subjected to great pressure its action is almost exactly similar. There is a constant yielding to pressure which permits the gradual flow of glaciers, and exactly as in a river the flow is more rapid in the center than at the sides, and on the surface than at the bottom.

As the ice descends over the rough, rocky bed it becomes cracked and split into long tongues, or perhaps pinnacles, if the cracks happen to cross each other. The long fissures are called crevasses, the pinnacles seracs. The water melted from the ice finds its way through the crevasses and wells to the bed of boulders below, and passes to the outside air. Often very beautiful circles of ice are formed where the principal streams flow out. The earth and boulders which are carried down on the ice collect in moraines at the foot of the glaciers. Sometimes these piles are hundreds of feet in height. Many beautiful examples may be seen among the glaciers of the Selkirks.

In following down over the snow of the glacier a point is finally reached at which the snowfall is less than the annual melting, and below this point there is nothing but clear ice. This is called the dry glacier. The length of the dry glacier, and the distance the forefoot extends into the valley of course vary with the time of year, the snow line being lower in winter than in summer, and the forefoot extending much further into the valley in spring than in fall.

But apart from this there is often a melting away of the forefoot of the glacier more rapidly than the fresh ice from above comes down to take its place. At the present time this gradual recession seems to be common to nearly all observed glaciers in temperate climates. Indeed there is reported to be but one well authenticated case where the ice is really advancing into the valley. Many of the glaciers in Switzerland have had observations made upon them to show exactly the rate of flow and recession, but in this comparatively unexplored region but little work has been done, and it is with the object of recording in this Scrap Book one or two interesting facts that this entry is made.

Our first visit to Glacier was during the 15th, 16th and 17th of July, 1887. This was the first season the chalet had been opened, the only trail was a very poor one to the forefoot of the Great Glacier, and the bridges consisted of bare logs across the Asulkan and Illecillewaet creeks. On the day after our arrival we visited the glacier, taking a number of photographs. Upon examining one of these a few days ago attention was called to a great rock in the foreground which was partly buried in the forefoot of the ice. By a comparison of the markings on the great rock, and the position of certain trees on a neighboring ridge in respect to Sir Donald, the rock was identified without a doubt, and also the exact position of the camera when the view was taken. Here then is a record of the position of the ice almost exactly eleven years ago. This rock may be seen on the left just as one emerges from the trail and descends to the flat moraine. It will be easily identified by the markings, a copy of which is as follows:

/ Edge of ice
/ VII—16—1887

The most casual comparison of this rock with the present forefoot of the ice will show that the glacier is slowly but steadily retiring up the mountainside. From markings found painted on a number of rocks in the moraine it would appear that every year the forefoot recedes from twenty-five to forty-five feet. This amount of course is not constant as the weather and snowfall are very important factors, and vary considerably from year to year. Indeed there is reason to believe that within the past ten years the ice advanced for a short period, and then fell back, leaving its mark on a small moraine on the otherwise nearly flat boulder floor.

Any lover of nature will find the study and exploration of glaciers a most fascinating pastime; especially in this region where everything is so new and unknown the investigations will become doubly valuable from a scientific standpoint, and the student will have the satisfaction of knowing that he is treading in steps but seldom attempted by others and among scenes which can hardly be surpassed in any part of the world.

William S. Vaux Jr.
Bryn Mawr Pennsylvania, U.S.A.

Forefoot of the Illecillewaet Glacier, July, 1887.

The line on the rock indicates the edge of ice in 1887, August 25, 1898.

Aug. 28, 1898

The many attractions at Glacier will doubtless puzzle the traveller who for the first time visits this most charming of spots. A few words of general advice therefore may not be out of place here.

The Great Glacier of the Illecillewaet

The Glacier will doubtless first claim attention. It may be better to visit it in the afternoon as the light is then more attractive upon it, and if any photographing is to be attempted, no pleasing effects can probably be gotten before noon. The distance actually to the ice is about 1½ miles, & it will take 45 minutes or an hour to reach it. The first stream crossed is the Asulkan, after leaving which the path keeps close to the Illecillewaet till the moraine is reached. The return trip will occupy 30 to 45 minutes.

Lake Marion & Mt. Abbott

Another trail starting from the south end of the Annex leads to Lake Marion & thence to Mt. Abbott. The lake is about 1750 ft. above the hotel, & the distance is less than 2 miles. On the way up exquisite views of Eagle Peak & Sir Donald are had through the trees, whilst a trail skirting the north end of the lake leads to Observation Point whence superb views of Rogers Pass & the Loop Valley are obtained, with the silver thread of the Illecillewaet, flanked by the railroad, winding through the latter.

Mt. Abbott

The ascent from the lake to the summit of Mt. Abbott should be made by everyone at all equal to the exertion of a day's climb. For a description of this trip the reader is referred to the article by Dr. J. H. Stallard. With the improved condition of the trail this year, it is probable that with an early start—say 5 a.m. at the latest—the ascent may be more satisfactorily made in a single day.

Cascade & Mt. Avalanche

Another excellent trail is that to the top of the Cascade, & thence to the grassy slopes which culminate in the fine twin peak of Mt. Avalanche. The view is a superb one when the points outlined against the sky just above the snowsheds are reached, & in many respects rivals that from Mt. Abbott, though it is not so extensive. The most striking object is perhaps Mt. Sir Donald, which rises as a great square pyramid. Two sides of it are visible, & thus presents an extremely different aspect from that seen from any other point. From an elbow about halfway up Mt. Cascade where the trail reaches its most southern point, a fine view of the "Great Glacier" & its rough icefall is had, & throughout where it can be seen through the trees, the Asulkan Valley is most exquisitely beautiful. This trip should have a day devoted to it if possible, & the visitor is strongly urged on this, as on the other more extended trips, to make an early start. The morning light discloses beauties not dreamed of, & should the weather be warm, as it sometimes is, one gets the advantage of doing the harder part of his work in the cool of the day. An early breakfast & a substantial lunch are always obtainable without difficulty.

Asulkan Pass

Possibly the most charming of any of the trips is that up the Asulkan Valley. This gem of alpine beauty was first explored in 1888 by Wm. S. Green,* F.R.G.S. whose "Among the Selkirk Glaciers," published in 1890, will be found an agreeable companion. It contains an excellent map, a new edition of which corrected to date would be invaluable. The name Asulkan given by Mr. Green to this valley, with the glacier & pass at its southern end, is the Indian name for the mountain goat, really a variety of antelope.

The Asulkan Valley is hemmed in on its easterly side by Glacier Crest, & the ridges running from it to the southward which form the western side of the great Illicillewaet Névé, or snowfield. On its western side the valley is bounded by the long range which is comprised in order beginning at the north, of Mt. Abbott, The Rampart, The Dome, Pollux and Castor. A series of glaciers sweeps down from all of these except Abbott, & the streams flowing from them form a number of most graceful & beautiful waterfalls, the Seven Falls, so far unnamed in detail, but which at other places would be considered worthy of special attention. The rich meadows would prove tempting pastures for herds of cattle or flocks of goats, notwithstanding bear tracks are frequently seen there. At the distance of about 2½ or 3 miles the river is contracted between narrow rocky walls, & the cañon sides here show no striking signs of glacial action.

**William Spotswood Green (1847-1918), an Irish cleric, was persuaded to visit the mountain regions of Canada by his cousin Henry Swanzy. Swanzy had been on the British Association for the Advancement of Science excursion to the end of the CPR track (Kicking Horse Pass) in 1884, then continued by horse along the proposed rail route to the coast. In 1888 Green and Swanzy explored much of the area south of the rail line around Glacier House.*

Emerging from the gorge the path leads over an old moraine, across the stream flowing in from the east, and then up a very steep grassy slope to the shack erected this year for the accommodation of tourists. This point is about 2000 ft. above Glacier House, & about 5 miles distant from it. From about this level superb views of the Asulkan Glacier are had, whilst the glacier-covered sides of Castor & Pollux, & The Dome are exceedingly striking. The ice towers, pinnacles, obelisks, minarets & turrets are of surpassing grandeur & beauty, & the sight of them is an ample recompense to anyone who takes this trip, which in fact includes more variety than any of the others now easily accessible. Looking from near the shack to the north, the Hermit Range is most beautifully set out whilst nearer at hand and passing eastward come in order the twin peaks of Mt. Avalanche, Eagle Peak & Sir Donald, the latter manifesting quite a different aspect from what we have before seen.

From the shack the ridge may be followed upwards for a mile or more, till sufficient elevation is obtained to observe the peaks of the Dawson Range. The total distance of the round trip is some 12 or 14 miles, & the time occupied about the same number of hours.

A variation of this trip is to follow upwards along the crest of the great moraine just east of the glacier, instead of climbing the grassy slopes to the shack. Later the névé is crossed to the Asulkan Pass proper.

Glacier Crest

The trip to Glacier Crest is not so often taken, but the view from the summit is said to be well worth the excursion.

The Loop

Other obvious walks are those along the railroad to "The Loop," & to the snowsheds, whence the changing panoramas of peaks are ever new and ever attractive. The view of Mt. Bonney which lies to the south of Ross Peak as seen from the top of "The Loop" is very beautiful.

The visitor who spends a week or more will have his time pretty fully occupied if he includes all of the foregoing, & he will then find other & new fields for his investigations, these notes being intended only as suggestions for the newcomer.

George Vaux Jr.
404 Girard Bldg., Philadelphia

A *note to photographers!*

Take care you don't *over* expose. The light is *wonderfully actinic.*

Glacier House staff, guides, waiters, and cook, August 16, 1899.

Mt. Abbott
Sept. 5, 1898

We appreciate greatly the high value of this record of experience. After what has been so well said already about the ascent of this mountain it may seem superfluous to add anything further. The account referred to, however, does not mention the fact that the summit of the central ridge or shoulder of Mt. Abbott involves in itself an interesting climb & is a point from which a panorama of the mountains and glaciers on all sides may be obtained.

The ascent to this point may be made in about three hours & descent in 1½ to 2. Take the trail to Marion Lake & follow it until you reach the grassy slopes immediately below the northern end of the mountains. Then strike across the boulders to the right and work round the north edge . . . & so on to the summit of the ridge. There is no distinct trail after leaving the grass slopes.

(This point was reached by three members of a party which left the hotel at 9 o'clock on the morning of Sept. 5th 1898. No invidious distinction shall be made here by mentioning the names of those who reached the summit & those who remained upon the lower "benches" in spite of the frequent application of the "stick." Suffice it to say that the climbers were guided by a lady & that the following ladies & gentlemen formed the party. Mrs. Schäffer, Mrs. W. Nesbitt, Mr. Bell-Smith, the Rev. T.F. Griffith & Dr. Ely.)

[Anon]

Lookout Mountain
Sept. 10, 1898

A party composed of the following persons ascended to Glacier Crest. Mrs. Dr. Schäffer, Mrs. Nesbitt, Miss Reid, Mr. Nesbitt and Mr. F.M. Bell-Smith with two porters. The trail up to the timber line is steep but well defined and the summit was reached in three hours. Here the artist Mr. Bell-Smith stopped to paint while the rest of the party continued on to the crest. Several very successful photographs were made by Mrs. Schäffer notably one overlooking the Glacier, the crevasses being seen to great advantage from this point. The weather was very fine and warm, the sky being almost cloudless.

[Anon]

Eagle Peak
Sept. 19, 1898

I have spent a very pleasant week at this hotel, & nothing could exceed the kindness & attention I have received from Miss Mollison* & the rest of the staff. My only climb was Eagle Peak, which, the guide being unwell, I had to do alone. I could obtain no information from anybody as to any portion of the route, so the following notes may be useful. Ascend to the top of the 2nd Cascade (a trail might with advantage be cut to this point)—follow the stream up the valley to small glacier at the head of the latter. Turn to left up rock and stone slopes; follow long straight couloir up to final rocks. Bear slightly to the right, & an easy but amusing scramble takes you to the summit. The view is superb. The ascent should take 5-6 hours, & for fairly good mountaineers is not difficult or dangerous, though it appears to be rarely attempted. A lantern should be always taken.

It seems a great pity that more facilities are not afforded to would-be climbers in this delightful district. If more competent guides for rock and ice work were obtainable, Glacier House would soon be a popular centre for mountain excursions. I would also suggest that the C.P.R. authorities should provide a big telescope with stand etc., of the type familiar in Alpine hotels. Such things are always popular.

Hugh E.M. Stutfield*
6 Charles St., Berkeley Square, London W.

**Jean Mollison managed Glacier House from 1897 through 1899 when Julia Young took over and managed the hotel for the next twenty years. Jean Mollison and her sister Anne had managed all three of the CPR's original mountain hotels, Mount Stephen House at Field, Glacier House, and Fraser Canyon House at North Bend.*

**Hugh E.M. Stutfield (1858-1929) was a British climber who travelled to Canada on two major mountaineering expeditions in 1898 and 1902. He participated in a number of first ascents and was a member of the group that first discovered and explored the Columbia Icefield. The book* Climbs and Explorations in the Canadian Rockies *(1903), which he coauthored with J. Norman Collie, is a classic work on early mountaineering in North America.*

June 22, 1899

I came here yesterday meaning to leave for the west today, but much knocking about the world has taught me the wisdom of devoting a little extra time to the enjoyment of a really charming place when I am fortunate enough to find it; so "today" has come, the train has come and gone, and I am still happy in the thought that my kind hostess, Miss Mollison, will for another day at least, make me forget that there is aught in this world but such sweet content at Glacier.

This morning two Toronto gentlemen, Mr. H. Sutherland and Mr. J.C. McCarthy, came out of the West, and together we made up a party to go over the Great Glacier, taking the two Swiss guides* with us. Of course, properly speaking, they took us with them. How shall I describe the glory of that climb: We went over the great field of ice, snow-covered as it was, and up beyond, and to the top of Glacier Crest. We really seemed to have climbed a mountain behind the Crest; for, from where we were, we could not see Glacier House, owing to a lower crest intervening. The climb was very steep, over snow all the time; and the marvellous accuracy of the Swiss guides was startlingly demonstrated by the discovery of several snow-covered crevasses.

Coming down the side of the mountain before we struck the glacier we had two wildly exhilarating slides. Several hundred miles a minute was the rate; and had the snow run on smooth and unruffled by such trifles as glaciers, thousand-ton rocks, and insidious crevasses, we should have, in probability, shot on by the hotel and missed the soul-warming lunch our waiting hostess had in ambush. Snow is a difficult thing to walk over when it is spread out on the flat; but miles of it tipped at the same angle as a snow-face is only possible with a Swiss Guide at either end of a line and oneself firmly looped in the middle—that's a fairly honest statement of the feeling of the three men of our party today.

**The CPR began hiring Swiss guides in 1899 in response to the suggestions and pressures of a number of the Glacier House visitors. The first year Edouard Feuz, the chief guide in the Interlaken district, was hired along with his friend Christian Häsler. They returned in 1900 with three more guides, four working at Glacier House and one at Mount Stephen House at Field, B.C. Between 1899 and 1912 up to twenty different guides worked for the company at its mountain hotels.*

To you, my friend, I may say, & without wishing to give offence, if the minister has not convinced you that you are really of subordinate interest in the scheme of creation, go up there to God's pulpit, without its cloth of scarlet—with nothing but the golden gleam of the sunshine and the snow-shroud, stretching away to the million-spaced blue, and take solemn thought with yourself. If you come away and still think that things in this world should be shoved around to make room for you, your fate in the future is appalling.

I can't give any scientific data as to the more or less rapid progress of the Glacier—and considering the importance of the subject this is really too bad and most unfortunate, though I may say it appeared to be coming up the mountain side toward us at an alarming rate when we were mixed up in that slide affair,—but I can say that we have had a most astonishingly good time—what would be called in India a "bally good time"; and mountain climbing is A.1., and the hotel is a bally good hotel, and Sir William Van Horne has the biggest show on earth out here and knows how to run it—there!

W.A. Fraser
Georgetown, Ont., Canada

(a later comment)
July 24, 1902

After nearly three years have elapsed I have read Mr. Fraser's account of the day's sport and gladly subscribe to all of it excepting the glissade at several hundred miles a minute as I am certain it was not faster than *one hundred* miles per minute.

J.C. McCarthy
Toronto, Ont.

Lost

Mr. Brown: last seen in the year ____ by ____________ in the company of Cheops, "The Hermit," and Sir Donald. In appearance Mr. Brown is very tall—taller than either of his boon companions. When last seen he was wearing a white hat, grey hair, a high white collar, and was dressed in heather mixture tweed. His feet were encased in boots much covered with mud, and showing evidence of much rough usage. A search party spent several days looking for the aged gentleman, but up to the present no trace of him has been discovered. It is feared that the hikannie (spirit) maidens have stolen him away. A large reward will be paid for definite information as to his whereabouts.

By Order
W.A. Fraser

July 23, 1899

Ye rocky, snow-clad peaks, towering so high
That clouds oft times enfold you: Ye hold in your embrace
Glaciers unknown and fields of ice unmeasured, that feed
The constant torrents rushing down your rugged sides,
That seem, in the far off, like crystal threads
Woven in rich and varied green that clothe your base.
From the dark recess of this deep ravine
How grand and wonderful do you appear.
But he who's bold enough to climb your giddy heights—
A Bryant or a Steel—sees from your summits
A sea of peaks beyond as far as eye can reach, and beholds
Natures magnificence in all its glory.

[Anon]

The First Ascent of Mt. Dawson Aug. 13, 1899

I take pleasure in entering in this Register a few minutes concerning the first ascent of Mt. Dawson from Glacier House as a base, which was made by Professor H. C. Parker* of Columbia University and myself, accompanied by Swiss guides Christian Häsler and Edouard Feuz on the 13th of August 1899.

The ascent of a peak so remote, should properly take three days; one to reach a suitable camping place at the base, one for the ascent, and a third for the return to the hotel. Our party took but one and one half days, and made a correspondingly forced march.

Leaving Glacier House at 12:40 on Saturday, August 12 we made a leisurely ascent to the Asulkan Pass, which we reached at five o'clock. The day was perfect, and the view of the Fish Creek Valley, and the fine glacier-bearing peaks in the southwest (not to speak of the near view of Mounts Fox, Dawson and Donkin) was most impressive. Spending a few moments only here, we began the descent of the extremely steep further slope of the Pass. Unlike this side, snow descends but a short distance, after which comes a considerable expanse of "Alp," and finally a very precipitous descent of over 1000 feet through a thicket of dwarf spruce, alder, hellebore, and the usual growths of wet slopes in these regions, landing one at length, at the margin of the Geikie Glacier. The entire descent is some 1700 feet. The passage across the Geikie Glacier, here possibly 1000 feet wide, was made without serious hindrance from crevasses, after which we proceeded up the wooded slope to the left (east) of the stream flowing from the Dawson Glacier, and at 7:20 pm found a suitable place for a bivouac at a point some 400 feet above the Geikie Glacier and close by the great moraine of the Dawson Glacier.

Leaving this camp at 3:55 A.M. we took at once to the moraine, and in but an hour (4:50) reached its upper end, 1280 feet above our starting point. While upon this upper section we observed the beautiful spectacle of the rising sun upon the mists drifting about Mts. Dawson and Donkin, from which we drew no favourable omen for continued good weather. The Dawson Glacier, shrunken and foul with mud and debris, had been constantly on our right. Beyond the moraine we entered the great amphitheatre between Mts. Dawson and Fox, and began the long ascent of the névé. The end of the gorge is formed by the arête joining Fox and Dawson—a rock wall some 600 feet high at its lowest point. At its base we made our second breakfast at 6:55, at an elevation of 2960 feet above our camp; this height we had made in just two hours.

The route chosen by our guides, apparently the only feasible one from the north, was by way of this arête to the great snow field that clothes the high slopes of Dawson on its northerly side, and thus, over snows, to the highest peak. The aneroid gave a reading of 3530 feet above camp for the low point of the arête. To reach it had required some of the most tedious climbing of the day, as the rocks were bad, and covered with a moist, sliding, disintegrated shale. Fully one and one half hours were spent in making these six hundred feet.

The arête itself was easy, yet offering a few ugly places, by reason of the steepness and slipperiness of the rock upon the right, with steep new snow on the left. The upper snows were reached at 9:25 at an altitude of 4450 feet above camp.

From here on it was a superb snow climb, at first with gentle ascent, then more steep, till coming under the rocks, that form the easterly end of the final peak, the snow sweeps up at an angle of 45 degrees to 60 degrees broken by our broad schrund around which we had to pass. The passage from snow to rock had to be made with great caution. The last few hundred lateral feet were over rock alternating with ice and snow arêtes. The summit was reached at 10:45 and appeared to have a probable altitude of 10,800 feet.

The day had not improved as we advanced. Low drifting vapors were weaving and parting about the vast array of alpine summits, that on a clear day would form an incomparable alpine panorama from this exalted view point. We enjoyed what magnificence the clouds would permit, and their own grand spectacle. Little opportunity was afforded for the use of the pocket level. The more westerly peak of Mt. Dawson proved to have almost identically the same height, yet with a few feet in favor of our own.

*Herschel Clifford Parker (1867–1944), the head of the Department of Physics at Columbia University and an avid mountaineer, was a founding member of the American Alpine Club. He made a number of first ascents in the Lake Louise vicinity around the turn of the century and instituted a personal survey of the mountains along the Great Divide north of the CPR line. He was one of the pioneer alpinists to attempt an ascent of Alaska's Mount McKinley.

Mount Dawson and the Dawson Glacier from the Asulkan Pass, Sept. 3, 1904.

Häsler and Feuz built a substantial stone-man in which we deposited a glass bottle containing a few of the items here set forth.

We left the summit at 11:40 a.m. and reached camp at 3 p.m. where we passed a half hour in packing up our belongings. The ascent of the Asulkan Pass, abominably tedious after such a day's work, was begun at 4:10 p.m. being rendered the more unpleasant by a drizzling rain that continued nearly all the way to the top. The only enlivening episode was the sight of a large goat on the opposite side of the ravine, possibly a mile distant. He remained in plain view some ten minutes, refusing to betray the interest in us that we were taking in him. At last, seeming to sight us, he moved rapidly away.

The top of the pass was reached at 6:30, but it was filled with a dense mist. The welcome change of grade was the principal evidence of our being beyond it. From here I think it may be said, we *hurried* over the snow, and availing ourselves of opportunities for glissades on the steep slope above the "shack," we made our descent as far as this structure in twenty minutes, the path at the Cañon was entered at 7:30, and at 8:45 the welcome lights of this delightful hotel came in view.

Too much praise cannot be awarded to the two guides for their masterly management of the ascent. Nearly every variety of climbing was presented, and in every sort their skill and utter reliability was manifested.

In view of this being their first ascent of a virgin peak in the Selkirks, we would recommend that the peak of Mt. Dawson reached by us be known as the Häsler Peak, and its companion (the equally high peak lying perhaps one third of a mile to the westward) the Feuz Peak. These splendid specimens of their craft deserve a lasting memorial in these scenes which they are rendering accessible to so many.

Note: It may not be out of place to say that one of the party was seriously out of condition at starting, and so remained until reaching the top of the arête. Whether from the inspection of the view, or for a reason of a more prosaic sort—the abandonment of his rucksack—an improvement here set in, which proved permanent.

Yet more interesting may be the impression of the guides as to the comparative difficulty of Mt. Dawson, and certain other well known peaks. They class it as hard as Sir Donald, more difficult than the Swiss Matterhorn, and similar to the Wetterhorn.

Charles E. Fay*
Tufts College, Massachusetts

Fay Party at Lake Louise, August 7, 1897. Front row, left to right, Charles S. Thompson, Charles E. Fay, Harold B. Dixon (seated), J. Norman Collie, unknown, and Peter Sarbach, the guide. The three unidentified men are A. Michael, C.L. Noyes, and H.C. Parker, mix and match. This group made the first ascent of Mount Lefroy at Lake Louise.

**Charles Ernest Fay (1846-1931) was a professor of mathematics and modern languages as well as Dean of the Graduate School at Tufts College, Massachusetts. He was one of the most prominent of early American alpinists, being a founder and president of both the Appalachian Mountain Club and the American Alpine Club. He brought some of the first American mountaineers to western Canada and participated in a number of first ascents in both the Rockies and Selkirks between 1894 and 1904.*

Glacier House Aug. 20, 1899

During the year which has intervened since I last wrote in this minute book, Glacier has lost none of its charms.

Guides

The most notable improvement has been the bringing here of the two Swiss guides. Thoroughly safe, and competent in every particular, there is afforded to the general visitor the opportunity to get a true insight into the attractions which mountaineering affords. The visit to the Illecillewaet Glacier may now be supplemented by a trip onto the ice itself under the guidance of Feuz or Häsler, which cannot fail to delight with its beauty and novelty. Entire confidence may be reposed in the guides, the chief requirement being an implicit obedience of their directions.

Mt. Abbott

The trip to Mt. Abbott is now made in 5 or 6 hours, owing to the trail having been extended and the skill of the guides.

Mt. Avalanche

For anyone anxious to make a real alpine ascent Mt. Avalanche is strongly recommended. Following up the ridge as referred to earlier, the glacier and snow field are crossed and the ridge ascended about midway between the two rocky peaks visible from the top of the Cascade. The arête is gained by typical rock climbing, and then followed to the summit which is probably 9500 to 9600 feet above sea level.

Superb View The view is indescribably grand and very extensive. A complete panorama of snowy mountains is unfolded, the Rockies to the eastward across the broad Beaver Valley, bounded on its further side by the rounded Prairie Hills. To the westward and southward are the Selkirks in equally vast and snowy array, whilst nearer are the beautiful Mt. Bonney, the range hemming in the Asulkan Valley on the west, the Mt. Dawson Range, & the Illecillewaet Glacier and snow field. Close at hand to the southeast is the magnificent pyramid of Mt. Sir Donald as the culmination of the whole, flanked as it is by Uto and Eagle Peak. This view must be seen in order to have the slightest appreciation of it. The ascent requires 12-13 hrs. for the round trip.

Illecillewaet Glacier Our observations on the Illecillewaet Glacier have been continued this year. Probably owing to the cool season the recession this year has been only about 16 feet. We have also taken the preliminary steps for measuring the rate of flow, but have no results to announce as yet.

Snowfall The most striking change in the whole district is the unusually large amount of snow yet remaining on the mountains. This is partly due to the abnormal snow fall of last winter—51 feet on the level of Glacier House—and partly to the unusually cold summer. In this connection it is interesting to note that snow fell here on the morning of Tuesday, August 15th, sufficient in amount to whiten the grass in the lawn. At Lake Louise there were 16 inches on the level.

George Vaux Jr.
404 Girard Bldg. Philadelphia, Pa.

Mount Sir Donald from summit of Mount Avalanche, August 7, 1899.

Aug. 24, 1899 Permit an American to record this appreciation of the enterprise of the Canadian Pacific Railway in having made this wonderful mountain region accessible to the public; in having established such a comfortable inn, so perfectly adapted to enjoyment of the scenery, and so admirably appointed and conducted. In a period of American travel of over 25 years we have found nothing in better keeping and character. For two days we have experienced the greatest pleasures out-of-doors and indoors. The easy means of access to the superb scenery, great natural wonders such as snowpeaks, eternal glaciers, commodious trails to the tops of the mountains, all provided for our comfort and security, stamps our Canadian brothers as our equals in enterprise and public spirit. . . The work done by several artists whose pictures in oil and water colors prove that this is a region surprisingly rich in material for study from the artist's stand-point. The works of two favorite artists Mower Martin and Bell-Smith,* both members of the Royal Canadian Academy, are especially commendable "to the public." These gentlemen spending weeks in these mountains doing for the Selkirks what Bierstadt did for the Sierra Nevadas. This is the most satisfactory resort for the artist, the photographer, the lover of nature, the seeker for the grand and beautiful, as on no transcontinental railway can be found crowded together such an aggregation of scenic grandeur.

[Anon]

Sept.6, 1899 Topside that hill Maker call 'um Malian Lake, any man can catches number one handsome Looksee.

Jas. N. Sullivan
Shanghai, China

**Frederick Marlett Bell-Smith (1846-1923) came to eastern Canada from England in 1866. An accomplished landscape painter who worked mainly in watercolours and oils, he supported himself as a photographer (1867-74) and illustrator, and eventually taught art in St. Thomas, London and Toronto, Ontario. He was assisted by the CPR to paint the Rockies in 1887 and 1890, and he made numerous privately funded trips west, often travelling with Thomas Mower Martin (1838-1934). Martin was another landscape painter from England who had come to Canada in 1862. Primarily self-taught, he was also noted for his watercolours and oil paintings. He was the first director of the Ontario government art school.*

July 11, 1900 The Third Ascent of Mount Sir Donald was made July 11th 1900 by the undersigned with Edward Feuz & Charles Schlunegger as guides.

We left Glacier House at 2:40 A.M. just as the dawn was breaking & proceeded rapidly up the trail to the Glacier & across to the foot of the small glacier* coming down from Sir Donald on the West, reaching the mountain itself at an elevation of about 9000 ft. shortly before 8 o'clock.

We had considerable difficulty in getting from the névé on to the rocks owing to some enormous bergschrunds which blocked our progress. Finally after an hour's delay a feasible route was discovered involving however a very dangerous traverse across a nearly perpendicular snow field which fell away below us into the yawning cavern of the great crevasse, lined with icicles as with teeth. This accomplished, we zigzagged up the southern part of the western side of the mountains, in full view of the Glacier House till the arête was reached a little way above the almost perpendicular break plainly seen in the southern arête. Our progress was considerably interfered with by very soft fresh snow, into which we sank to our knees, & which was constantly slipping from its underlying ice. The arête was gained at 11 o'clock, the elevation being about 9600 ft. From this point we climbed steadily to the summit, carefully avoiding the fine, icicle-lined, snow cornices descending from mountains on its eastern flank, & at 12:35 p.m. set foot on the actual summit, a small ridge of quartzite but 4 or 5 ft. long & with a gentle snow slope extending from it for a few feet to the north & east. Here we found the cairn or "stone man" left by former climbers & added our own record to those already deposited there.

The views were superb in every direction, a vast sea of snowy peaks, whilst between us & the Rockies was the charming Beaver Valley & opening to the south east the broad valley of the Spillimacheen.

The weather conditions on the summit were not at all ideal & the guides advised a rapid descent. The main summit is not visible from the Hotel, as it lies behind an outlying spur. We signalled from this to our friends below & at 1:25 left the summit which our barometer recorded as being 10,175 ft. The thermometer on the top stood at 48 degrees Fahr. Our elevation was thus shown as nearly 500 ft. lower than former observers, tho this is not to be strictly depended on as the barometer had been acting somewhat erratically.

We had scarcely left the summit when the storm broke on us in all its fury. Sleet, rain & hail, & familiar snow but in great quantities. The wind rushed violently, now up, now down, now across our path. The whole mountain was strongly electrified, & each shrill crack of thunder would be preceded by a sharp buzzing from the points of our ice axes. In one hour & five minutes, at 2:35 p.m., we reached the point where we had gained the arête. The wet condition of the rocks, the falling snow & ice, loosened by the rain & wind made extreme caution necessary. Once we stopped & rested for about 15 min. under an overhanging crag, which protected us from the fusillade from above. The storm now abated, we could see the sun shining. Finally after a very careful traverse of the vertical snow field above the bergschrund, where we all went with our "faces to the wall," the snow being very treacherous, we subsequently reached the névé again at 5:15 & in 35 min. after some exhilarating glissades reached the moraine at the foot of the small glacier. It was then easy work to get back to Glacier House which we reached in good condition at 7:15 p.m., having spent a very satisfactory 16 hours & a half in the undertaking.

Notwithstanding the difficulties, there was not a moment when the guides did not appear to be perfectly at home & familiar with their duties. Their skill & knowledge of their craft are unsurpassed.

I have been asked what struck me most in the view. There were two things: one, the sense of our unequalled elevation, for no near peak appeared to be anywhere near so high; and the other the vast extent of the névé & Glacier of the Asulkan, which far exceeded what I had supposed it to be after a careful study of it.

George Vaux Jr. of Philadelphia
member Appalachian Mountain Club

Although this was called Green's Glacier before 1905, A. O. Wheeler suggested that a glacier more closely associated with Mr. Green be so named and that this be called the Vaux Glacier.

View south from summit of Mount Sir Donald, July 4, 1900.

Aug. 4, 1900

For the benefit of the unmarried ladies who visit this section we have caused model husbands to be placed on "Sandwich Island," Glacier Crest, and Avalanche Crest. They are warranted not to talk back and have no bad habits except that they will stay out nights. (For further particulars, see the wall bills).

As I am not a member of any Alpine Club, Scientific Society or kindred organization this levity may possibly be permitted.

Jamie R. Stern
Spokane

Sir Donald
Sept. 11, 1900

What was practically two ascents were made on Sept. 11th. I record the fact as a protest against the introduction of the very frequent Swiss practice (except amongst some really first-class guides) of always endeavouring to compel a climber to engage 2 guides to do the work of one. Charles Schlunegger, after a day right up the Great Glacier with rock scramble then to Lookout Mountain (a very enjoyable & easy expedition), consented to take my brother & me up Sir Donald: but was met with opprobrium from the other guides, as in previous ascents two had always been engaged. We declined two as unnecessary, & would have tried it guideless when a compromise was effected. Mr. G.G. Butter was desirous of climbing the mountain, so the guides agreed that he with Ed. Feuz should accompany us, keeping in touch throughout. Hereby the guides assented to the principle of two dangers making one safety, they having previously asserted that 3 on a rope (one a guide) was unsafe, two hopelessly so; yet thus they suggested to make the ascent. A second protest I wish to make is against the terrible difficulties & dangers impressed by the guides upon the poor climber as inseparable from the ascent. It is good for them: it is no doubt wise for the unskilled tourist: but it is very much exaggerated. Given *fine weather*, fair mountaineering abilities, some experience of climbing without guides, & the peak in pretty good condition, & the expedition would be infinitely preferable without guides at all. But please note the provisos. . . .

To sum up: The dangers, at most, are of extremely small importance: avalanching with 3 on a rope of decent length would nowhere do any harm on Sir Donald, as the snow patches are not extensive: iced rocks are of no real account: falling stones are a very off chance even by the stock route.

The main line is otherwise extremely obvious & excessively easy: broad ledges to saunter on & simple rocks are the staple product of the face climb; simple rocks continued & easy snow at a good angle from the point where the arête is struck to the summit. Variations ad lib. to taste can be made along the whole route & several interesting major deviations would, I believe, be of advantage in many ways to the energetic & experienced rock-climber.

James Outram*
Pitlochry, Scotland

The guides at Glacier House, Fred. Michel, Karl Schlunegger, Edouard Feuz Sr., and Jacob Müller, July 14, 1900.

**Sir James Outram (1864-1925) was an ordained minister of the Church of England, a graduate of Pembroke College, Cambridge. After serving the church for a number of years, he took up mountaineering to overcome failing health; following a brief apprenticeship in the Alps, he came to Canada in 1900 to climb in the Rockies. In 1901 and 1902 he completed a number of first ascents including Mount Assiniboine and several major summits near the Columbia Icefield. He lived in Canada for the remainder of his life and was an active member of the Alpine Club of Canada.*

Sir Donald
Sept. 12, 1900

I arrived at the Glacier House with my wife on Sept. 11th—from Vancouver after a week's stay on the coast.

The next day I ascended Sir Donald. Starting at 3:10 a.m. by the light of a half-moon we made a rather slow progress till dawn, a few light clouds & a huge ring round the moon presaging the bad weather which shortly followed. We went up the moraine to the left of the glacier, breakfasted near the foot of the rocks. From here we made good time (1¾ hrs.) to the top, arriving at 9 o'clock—5 hrs., 50 mins. from the hotel. There was much snow, & towards the summit the steps of Messr. Outram's party saved us time & labour. A long thin circle of cloud obscured the tops of the peaks along the main range—otherwise the panorama was perfect. We spent an hour on and about the summit, & returned to the hotel at 2 o'clock.

The impressions left by the peak on the minds of previous climbers appear to differ considerably. No doubt, judged by modern alpine standards, Sir D. is not a very terrible undertaking, but I cannot quite endorse all that Mr. Outram says as to its excessive ease, or agree with him that its rock ledges are suitable places to saunter on; and, as some sad experiences have taught me that holding mountains too cheaply is the most fertile source of alpine disasters, I should like to record my opinion that only thoroughly experienced & qualified amateurs ought to attempt the ascent without guides.

I forgot to mention that Jacob Müller & Friedrich Michel accompanied me, & that I was thoroughly satisfied with them. Müller, in particular, is not only very safe & careful, but possesses that knowledge of snow & ice which one expects from an Oberland guide.

Hugh E.M. Stutfield
Berkeley Square, London W.

Sept. 16, 1900

P.S. I note with satisfaction, not untinged, perhaps, with a dash of pardonable pride, the various improvements effected since my last visit two years ago, particularly the trails, now as big & safe as Piccadilly pavements; the guides who plant my trembling footsteps on the mountains; & last, not least, the noble telescope with its Heaven-kissing Pagoda.

And if, O potent divinities of the C.P.R., who have so courteously unbent to our previous supplications, you would only improve the weather a little during this unnecessarily moist September season—& likewise enlarge the shelters leading to the *annexe*, where now your memorialists pass to & fro on wet nights wading puddles & dodging waterspouts (& ice-axes) to their manifest discomfort, you would establish fresh claims upon our gratitude, & your petitioners will ever pray, etc., etc., etc.

[H. E. S.]

Illecillewaet Glacier and Glacier House.

Mount Dawson
July 16th, 1901

Left hotel July 15th with Ed. Feuz & Frederick Michel as guides. Crossed Asulkan Pass and descended upon the Geikie Glacier. (Fine aspect of Geikie Icefall noteworthy.) Spent the night in a cosy spot among the spruce trees a few hundred feet above the Geikie Glacier which we crossed.
comes from the Mt. Dawson group. From the moraine we stepped upon the névé which we ascended until we had nearly reached the bottom of the couloir which descends from the Mt. Dawson arête at the left of the peak as you face it. A diversion is necessary here to the rocks on the left which are climbed for a height of several hundred feet, thence by way of the couloirs to the saddle, between Mt. Dawson's summit and a subsidiary buttress on the left. Thence turning to the right by the principal arête to the summit itself.

From the saddle especial caution was necessary in our case because of the snow cornice which extended the whole length of the arête. The peak has properly two summits, the further or western one, about 1100 feet beyond the nearer one, the two connected by the narrow arête. The western summit we were the first to attain. My barometer made the height 11100 ft., which cannot be far out of the way. It is plainly higher than Sir Donald; this same barometer gave Mt. Stephen (at Field) as 10200 ft. which is, I believe, actually about correct, a little under perhaps.

The climb of Mt. Dawson is an extremely interesting one; it involves for the climber a variety of work, both on rocks, on snow slopes and on glacier. The view from the summit is undoubtedly quite as fine as from Sir Donald or any other of the Selkirk summits, and, rising as it does from such an amphitheater of its own wonderful group, as seen from the Asulkan Pass, this peak seems to me to be the most beautiful of any in this immediate region. No serious difficulties are met with for the amateur who has had a moderate amount of experience, but the best of judgement is called for from the guide in the event of the existence of a snow cornice upon the arête.

Our times were: left camp 3:20 A.M.
arrived summit 10:10 A.M.
left " 10:20 A.M.
arrived camp 2:00 P.M.

I failed to mention that the weather conditions were excellent, except just as we reached the summit when a severe snow squall beset us and obliged us to return immediately. The wind blew very fiercely, almost threatening our safe balance upon the arête, and the driving snow needles cut our faces painfully.

B. S. Comstock

The first ascent of Sir Donald by a lady. August 3, 1901

On Aug. 3rd 1901 my wife & self reached the summit: she thus being the first lady to accomplish the feat. Having done so much, she thinks that I should undertake the task of writing the account.

I may say that neither of us had done any mountain climbing before. My sole experience had been the ascent of Mt. Avalanche a few days before as experiment: hers had been confined to climbs to Avalanche Crest, the slopes below Mt. Abbott, & the summit of Asulkan Pass, & fossil beds on Mt. Stephen. We therefore made our attempt with some feelings of diffidence, not being able to derive much comfort from a perusal of the very different accounts of previous trips contained in the interesting Minute Book.

I may say however that we did not expect "the mere saunter over flat ledges" which one gentleman enjoyed: perhaps the road has been broken up a little since his trip! Anyway the rocks did not remind us much of the pavement of Piccadilly. Still, practised mountaineers no doubt look at these things with a more lenient eye than do mere novices. On the other hand we hoped to escape the dreadful storm & tempest mentioned in another account and in this we were indeed fortunate, the weather being perfect. On the whole we derived most comfort from Mr. Stutfield's calm & temperate account & certainly took to heart his advice "not to hold any mountain too cheaply."

We however held ourselves rather cheaply when we rose at the unearthly hour of 2 a.m. on the eventful morning.

We had only confided our secret to a chosen few, not being over-confident of success, but one or two others seemed to "smell a rat": one gentleman, in particular, asked me once or twice the day before whether we were going to try. I could reply with perfect truth that I was *thinking* of it: and I certainly *did* think hard during the day & night before.

Soon dressed, we made our way toward the kitchen, guided by a savoury smell of fried bacon and found the guides ready with an excellent breakfast, Clarke* being a great cook in addition to his other accomplishments. We cannot pretend to give a scientific account of our climb: words such as arête, couloir, névé, bergschrund etc. were unknown to us and for all we knew, might have been the names of ferocious animals which inhabit these mountains.

We had no barometer or thermometer, though the genial Mark Twain relates that he found the latter instrument very useful: he used to boil it! and as water boils at a lower temperature at great heights, he evolved the great theory that the higher you appear to be, the lower you really are!

We started at 3:15, my wife riding a pony kindly furnished by Mrs. Young, who did all in her power to help us. She was thus able to ride for nearly an hour, which was a great help. We started under a bright moon which about the time we passed the great glacier began to pale before the rival luminary. (N.B. I am *not* getting a penny a line). We left the pony about 4 and went steadily up the rest of the trail, or to the glacier of Sir Donald & up the snow slopes: here my wife slipped and fell, but only lost her axe, which careened gaily down for a long distance: however the ever-active Clarke soon retrieved it and caught us up in time for second breakfast at 7 o'clock on the snow, under the rocks of the great amphitheatre. . . . It was decidedly cold and we stayed 20 minutes, then started for the real work.

**Charles Clark was the son of an Englishman living in Switzerland who hired the first Swiss guides for the CPR. In 1899 he was interpreter for the guides in Canada. Becoming a fully certified Swiss guide, he worked at Glacier House for several years between 1900 and 1905.*

It took some little while to find a way from the snow on to the rocks, as the former had melted away somewhat: however Karl, by a little digging, soon made a fairly easy approach and we started on our "saunter." I suppose that to a mountaineer the rocks may be fairly easy, but to novices like ourselves some places seem quite unpleasant & ticklish, though we went on steadily that the actual exertion is not great. At one very wet place under the overhanging rocks I fell & slid gracefully on the prominent part of my waistcoat but was pulled up by my wife assisted perhaps by Karl who was leading. However we gained the arête (is that right?) without great trouble & went fairly easily up the snow, though we often went in leg-deep, it seemed at times that we were unpleasantly near the overhang of the snow and we tried not to think of how much or how little was underneath us, having no fancy for an involuntary glissade at an unpleasant angle for a mile or so: however we had complete and justified trust in our leader. We gained the real summit about 11:30 and after a short rest there, crawled slowly to the point whence we could see the hotel (and rather wished we were there).

We soon saw a flash of light from below and signalled back.

We tried to admire the view, but no one could take in such a view as lay all around us in the short time at our disposal. Others have tried to describe it: we give up the attempt. We saw more peaks "than you could shake a stick at" to use an expression of the late Artemus Ward. We remained on the peak till one o'clock, lunching & taking photos, but it was too cold for comfort.

We both thought the descent by far the worst part of the day, the great excitement being over: the rock climb seemed interminable and the snow field below seemed as if it would never get nearer. There was of course much more water coming down than in the morning and we had several drenching shower baths, but were fortunate in escaping the falling stones, though some fell before and behind us. We hurried as well as we could over the dangerous parts: at one nasty little place my wife had a bad slip, but needless to say was promptly pulled up to safety again in no time by the guides and this time she clung nobly to her axe otherwise it would have gone into the Lost Property Office. On the whole however she came down far better than her aged husband. We of course had many rests on the way down and reached the snow without further adventure, at least Clarke (leading) did, but when I set foot on it a large piece caved in and I began to wish I had lived a better life: however I only went a few feet down and in any case could not have gone farther as Clarke had the rope taut: my wife fell a short way into the hole, but scrambled out easily. We had one or two good glissades down the snow slopes, but when we got on the ice we all, including the guides, slipped & slid about in the most absurd manner: however, all danger being over, we could afford to laugh, though it was nearly annoying at times. The walk down the stones seemed the most tiring part of the day, but we soon reached . . . the Hotel at 7:15.

We found quite a crowd on our arrival and my wife was quite embarrassed by the kind & hearty reception when she rode on to the lawn.

I did not state that she was dressed for the occasion, in—er—well—certain nether garments of mine & puttees, as she thought that even the shortest skirt might be inconvenient or even dangerous. We cannot say too much in praise of our guides, Karl Schlunegger & Chas. Clarke, the former leading us up, the latter down: their care & skill made even us novices feel as safe as is possible to feel on a mountain side, where one seems rather like a fly on a wall.

Of course the danger of the falling stones cannot be guarded against and that is the most serious part of the climb. One gentleman writes that "the 100th or 1000th person might get hit" but why such very different shades of odds? However, he goes on to say "there is always the chance to reckon with" and so things will remain, unless some experienced climber like the writer referred to, can find a new line to avoid this danger. Hurrying over the dangerous parts is all one can do, but there is again the chance of hurrying into a shower, which by going slow, one might have avoided. Personally we have decided that once is enough. We of course were favoured with the best conditions of weather and of the rocks and advise all novices like ourselves, if they decide to chance the falling rocks, to hope for the same weather and the same two able & kind guides.

R. Berens
England

E. Evelyn Berens.

The first ascent of Mount Grizzly Aug. 31, 1901

Many gifted people have sadly wasted their talent in trying to get other people to rise early in the morning, promising them all kinds of good things. The most tempting of the baits being that early birds get worms. However, when you have tried to sleep a couple of hours on your wrong ear and have stepped out on the wrong side of the bed with the wrong foot first at half past two in the morning, you do not care for worms, neither do the immortal sayings of other mortal beings awaken your interest. The average man's humor is ugly and cynical on such occasions; and I am not above the average. Even the kindness of my companion in misery, the Reverend Dr. John E. Bushnell, of Minneapolis, U.S. I drew my attention to "beauty of the moon yielding to the rising sun"—I cite the exact words out of admiration, for the man, who so early in the morning can clothe his impressions in poetical garments, he is—well, I will say with Kipling "You're a better man than I am, Gunga Din." Even this kindness only produced in me a contrary desire to remark, that she usually did get the stuffing knocked out of her in the final round; but such is the power of good company, that the remark was never uttered.

When finally the sun has finished his disgraceful pugilistic feat, we reached the Rogers Pass, and took a trail running along the left bank of the river between the Mount Cheops and the Hermit range; this trail lasted about half a mile, and after scrambling along the bank for a painful quarter of an hour more, we crossed the river on a bridge, built for the occasion by our two guides, Carl Schlunegger and Friedrich Michel, and then we entered the dark and unexplored depths of the Selkirk underbrush.

The true character of a Selkirk underbrush has never to my knowledge been fittingly described, nor do I believe that it ever will be, seeing that no man likes to place himself on record as a rude, coarse, unrefined, blaspheming and vulgar person; also time, even a few hours, not to speak about a night's sleep, will throw a cloak of charity over his impressions. The only means of getting to the truth would be to lead a couple of men with a robust and unscrupulous craving for veracity through the bushes with a stenographer to take down their exclamations and impressions along the route. This is given as a suggestion in behalf of humanity and truth, but I would also advise, that the record be printed as a scientific essay, as the government would be likely to confiscate it as a purely literary product. To avoid misunderstanding, let me say that a stenographer would have been of no use in our party, as Mr. Bushnell would not willingly express his impressions, and I, out of respect for my companions,could not even if I would, so a record of our exclamations would have had no scientific value. It may be added, that the guides expressed themselves in the German language.

Although it does not seem possible, that any self-respecting animal should degrade itself to make such a place its home, I am sorry to say—with an apology to the grizzly bear, if I should be mistaken—that we saw ample testimony to the fact that this animal, not only used to board there and eat berries, but really also slept there in the night, its bed still being warm.

As everything must end, so did also the underbrush end, and the glory of emerging out upon grassy slopes and rocks and snow would inspire a man to anything from uttering blood-curdling Indian warwhoops to saying the prayers; I tried the first method; but my voice was not strong enough to rise to the occasion.

We had our second breakfast at 8 o'clock (we left Glacier House about ten minutes to 4 o'clock) on a grassy slope along a whispering brook, whose language we were never better able to appreciate, and enjoyed our cigarettes for half an hour.

Then there arose a most serious and perplexing question with which the guides never before had been confronted. The question was not along which route it would be possible to reach the summit but which of the many highroads we should honor with our attention and along which we should take our morning's constitutional. But as Swiss guides do not particularly care for morning constitutionals, very likely because they do not need them, they decided in the kindness of their heart to give us as much as they could for our money under the present unfavourable conditions, and took us straight up the narrow snow-couloir, running directly up to the top; after having gone ca. halfway up this we took to the rocks on the right side for the sake of variety, and so reached the top at 11:45 after a very easy ascent which hardly, with a few exceptions, could be called climbing; but which was the nearest we could get to it.

The view from the top was magnificent; but we were badly handicapped in enjoying it by a heavy smoky air.

After having gone through the ordinary routine of eating, snapping kodaks, building a "stone-man," and writing our names, we left the top about 1:30, had a few nice snowslides, drank from the various rivulets, showed the same linguistic good behaviour as in the morning and reached the Glacier House at 6:30 in the evening.

And so it came to happen, that we have the honor of having made the first ascent of Mt. Grizzly.

It's very likely, but our only chance, "honi soit qui mal y pense."

Aug. Eggers
Grand Forks, N. Dak. U.S.A.

August 31, 1901 Established a Triangulation and Photographie Station on the summit of Mt. Sir Donald.

Sept. 7th, 1901 Established a Triangulation and Photographie Station on the higher summit of the Swiss Peaks.

Arthur O. Wheeler* D.L.S.
Dept. of the Interior, Ottawa, Ont.

**Arthur Oliver Wheeler (1860-1945) was a major influence in the development of Canadian alpinism. A Dominion Land Surveyor, explorer and mountaineer, he worked mainly in the mountains of Canada. His two volume book* The Selkirk Range, British Columbia *details his photo topographical survey of the area in 1901 and '02 and is the first history of the Glacier House area. He also surveyed extensively in the Rockies, mapping six hundred miles of the Great Divide between 1913 and 1925.*

With Elizabeth Parker and J. C. Herdman he founded the Alpine Club of Canada in 1906. As well as being the club's first president, he was its leading force, managing director, and editor of the Canadian Alpine Journal *until the late 1920's.*

Abbott, Afton
July 7, 1902

Miss Kate Archer, G. F. Archer, and Edouard Feuz as guide ascended Mt. Abbott and then continued to Mt. Afton, put our names in bottle on this mountain. I myself, being anxious to explain our lateness to my mother, made the distance from Lake Marion to Glacier House in fifteen minutes; would not advise anyone coming down so quickly.

Avalanche
July 8, 1902

Edouard Feuz and myself ascended Mt. Avalanche; soft snow made walking very tiresome. We took our lunch in a place where there was an overhanging rock and where there was "standing room only." We put our names in a bottle at summit; view not very good as clouds were too numerous. Weather cleared when we were halfway down.

South Spur of Sir Donald
July 9, 1902

Miss Kate Archer and myself (G. F. Archer) made a trip to the southern spur of Sir Donald (I believe that this mountain has no name so have designated it as above for want of a better). The walk on the snow during the ascent was particularly tiresome as snow was very soft.

Our view was simply A No. 1, *this view should be missed by no one who cares for snow scenery*. After spending a few minutes on the summit we descended via the eastern slope and had a glorious slide, carrying along with us several tons of snow; I think it more truthful to say that the snow carried us along. We originally started guide first, my sister second and myself last but during the melée our positions were reversed. To make a long story short: after taking another slide and having a snowball form from the avalanche and strike my sister in the back (just as she was about to stop) nearly putting her out of sight (the ball was about two feet in diameter, consequently momentum was great), we reached the Glacier House in time to make away with two very substantial suppers.

George F. Archer, A.I.C.C.
New York City

July 11, 1902 Arriving at Glacier Hotel on the 4th inst. with my friend, I have spent a very pleasant week. Although it rained heavily when I came and continued to do so all the following day, I did not feel discouraged or let some good folks make up my mind to leave next day and see if the sun is not shining some other place further on. From the window of our delightful little sitting room I watched the wonderful mist clouds passing over the two splendid summits of Sir Donald and Eagle Peak; and I would say to those disheartened travellers who arrive here in wet weather and can only give vent to their feelings in grumblings that if they look up to the mountains and watch the wonder & beauty of the clouds passing over there they would, I think, find a pleasure that will make them confess that even in rain the rocky peaks heaving through the mists can look grand and even "awesome." The path up to Marion Lake I found easy and most delightful as it is under the pines all the way and shaded from the sun and the wooded surroundings are so pretty. I am no mountaineer, only a very ordinary walker, and I found this walk, also the one up the cascade on the hill opposite the hotel, and to the Great Glacier, comparatively easy. The enjoyment has been great, and I am sure everyone who comes to Glacier ought to spend some days so as to properly see the beauties of it. Some climbing I think is necessary if one wants to understand how fascinatingly beautiful the scenery is. The true grandeur of the mountains can hardly be understood by looking at them from the hotel.

Mary Gibson
Glasgow, Scotland

July 21, 1902 One thing I have noticed among these mountains is the red snow found in many places. Sometimes it is quite a brilliant scarlet color. Can anyone give an explanation of this? The Swiss guide did not know but said someone had told him it was *mosquitoes*! I suppose it is due to some animal or vegetable growth for it occurs in places where it is hard to see how any red colored rock dust could color it.

Irving Langmuir

August 6, 1902 The red snow is due to the presence of a tiny plant well known to botanists. Some specimens of red snow can be seen in Academy of Natural Sciences, Philadelphia, brought by Peary from one of his Arctic explorations.

E. M.

Mount Sir Donald and the Illecillewaet Glacier from Mount Abbott, Sept. 1, 1904.

Mt. Abbott
Sept. 17, 1902 Our ascent of this mountain was rather a novel one. Leaving the regular trail where it divides, about 300 feet above Marion Lake, we took the left-hand trail and followed it for perhaps a half mile until we reached a series of ledges on the right. Wishing to secure the more picturesque view of Sir Donald and the Great Glacier, we ascended these ledges going directly through the "bush" (this way is not recommended to ladies wearing friable skirts) until we reached the desired forest where we secured an excellent 8x10 photograph of the mountain and glacier with the forest in the foreground. There we continued up the steep slope, passing numerous mossy gullies, until we reached the "plateau," where we decided, instead of going down and following the usual trail, to attempt to scale the vertical cliff in front of us. At first sight this seemed impossible, but after traversing the rock fall and reaching the foot of the cliff we discovered a very easy succession of mossy ledges, in part forming a veritable stairway of rock, which brought us speedily to the large patch of snow on the shoulder of the mountain from which the way to the summit was simple. We came down by the regular trail, which we found awkward, tortuous & uninteresting. We decidedly recommend our trail-less method of ascent as vastly preferable in every way.

Asulkan Pass

This trip, up the charming Asulkan Valley to the foot of the Asulkan Glacier, thence through a delightful hillside park of Nature's own designing and where alpine flowers grow in profusion, to the moraine on the upper part of the glacier, thence traversing a mile or so of snow and ice to the summit of the pass from which we looked down into Fish Creek Valley with the glorious Dawson Range directly opposite, affords some of the grandest and most inspiring views to be had in this entire region. The trip is easily made, both in the amount of time and exertion required, though the assistance of a guide or of someone familiar with the route is necessary in the upper part of the glacier as fresh snow is likely to conceal the crevasses. No visitor to Glacier House should omit this trip who can possibly undertake it.

Avalanche Crest

This notable point of observation is within easy reach of the hotel and the trail is thoroughly admirable. No other excursion in the neighbourhood rewards the climber so abundantly, considering the slight extent of climb required. The best views are obtained from the lower portions of the "crest," as one gains nothing by climbing to the higher rocky arête—except a look down some awful precipices.

Eagle Crest

By this is meant the long sloping ridge leading from Eagle Peak in the direction of the hotel. It is easily reached by a steep climb along the edge of the "bush" to the right of the "meadow" above the cascade. Aside from other notable views, it gives an absolutely complete view of the Great Glacier from the top to "toe" without the least obstruction,—a peculiarity of no other viewpoint, so far as the writer is aware.

The Great Glacier

No one has really "seen" the glacier who has simply followed the trail to its foot. One needs to climb up on the ice and come into close proximity with its massive pinnacles of ice and yawning crevasses to get an adequate idea of its vastness. With the assistance of Clark, the guide, we climbed the lateral moraine to its highest limit and then crossed over on to the glacier, ascending a high knoll on the ice from which magnificent views were obtained. We would advise, from painful experience, that in addition to the usual outfit of spiked boots, rope and iceaxes, the climber take a stout pair of gloves to protect his hands from the sharp ridges of ice in climbing steep places.

H. W. Gleason*
E. W. Haruden.
Boston, Mass.

On the Asulkan Glacier, 1906.

**Herbert Wendell Gleason (1855-1937) was an accomplished landscape photographer and avid conservationist who travelled extensively throughout the American and Canadian west photographing wilderness and national park lands. Born in Massachusetts, he originally trained for the ministry and served as a pastor in the Congregational Church in Minnesota. In 1899 he retired from church work due to ill health, took up photography, and began his travels in the west. He was associated with a number of individuals who were active in the American national park movement and lectured throughout the eastern United States on the glories of the western parklands, his talks being illustrated by his own lantern slides which his wife had hand-coloured.*

Marion Lake and the Illecillewaet Valley July 10th, 1903

To those who have read the foregoing thrilling experiences of ascents to "Sir Donald" and other seemingly insurmountable peaks in this beautiful spot, this simple narrative will probably prove tame and uninteresting. If, however, your love of the beautiful and pastoral in nature has not been entirely overwhelmed by the stupendous and awe-inspiring majesty of the snow-capped peaks, take your staff in hand and follow the trail by easy ascents up to Marion Lake. They tell us it is three miles and should be walked in an hour & a quarter. You'll feel better to take an extra half or three quarters of an hour, however, and admire the beautiful views to be had of "Sir Donald" & Eagle Peak through the trees.

Once at the summit, a glance at the modest lake is sufficient, then press on to the "Observatory" a quarter of a mile further. Thousands of feet below to the left winds the beautiful Illecillewaet like a silver thread through one of the most indescribably charming and entrancing valleys the eye ever dwelt upon—and to the right, famous Rogers Pass. Fleecy clouds overhead, the sun shining brightly into the depths below, while the snow-capped peaks hold their eternal vigil as far as the sight can reach. "Fair as the garden of the Lord," refreshing to the spirit and a never-to-be forgotten impression of Infinity itself. No cloud without its silver lining—no mountain without its valley. Scale the peaks, if you will, and climb the glacier, but do not fail to take the trail to Marion Lake where the sun is shining and look over into the "Promised Land" just hidden by the haze enshrouding the "Delectable Mountains."

Robert Frothingham and wife
New York City

Avalanche Peak
July 26, 1903

We started from the Glacier House at 5 a.m. a party of three —Malcolm Stuart, New York City—Edward Feuz, jr., guide—and myself—with a slightly clouded sky but nevertheless with reasonable hopes for a fair day. The ascent was uneventful . . . . The "glissade" down the snow covered glacier furnished the only unusual event of the return. We were yet roped together, the guide ahead then S—, then myself.
Our course lay quite near the edge of the snow, where there were a number of small rocks imbedded as they had fallen from the mountain at the side, with their rough corners just showing. The guide cleverly steered his way through them unscathed, but poor S—, alas—! Yours truly, seeing the horrible example ahead had just time to steer off and escape.
The poet of the party offers the following:

A warning to men who glissade on their pants
Down glaciers and hills with very steep slants
The slide's very neat
But t'is hard on the seat
And makes all the pants look askance.

J. H. Batcheller

A group glissade, 1909. Photo by Bryon Harmon.

Fine Bathing in
Marion Lake
July 29, 1903

I am always on the lookout for a good chance to swim. On my first visit to Marion Lake it "looked good to me," but I felt doubtful about cold snow water. The next day I began investigations. I found the cold water running from the bathroom tap in the house—it comes from the cascade right opposite—scaled 48 degrees F. I took my thermometer up to the lake and found that was 61 degrees F. It was enough: I went in. Fine and bold water on a very fair beach, on the opposite side from outlet. Mosquitoes are somewhat bothersome but bearable.

J. H. Batcheller

Mount Tupper—
an unsuccessful start
July 30–31, 1903

Stuart and I wanted to try Mount Tupper for several reasons. We had heard it had never been climbed,—that is—to the knowledge of anyone of the Glacier House—and in addition to this easily satisfied thirst for notoriety we looked forward to camping out overnight upon its shoulder in the upper part of timberline. We left Glacier House at 2.30 p.m. July 30th, Edward Feuz, father—and son—Stuart and myself, with all our blankets, food, and camp equipment packed on a pony, and a boy to bring the horse back from the foot of the mountain. The walk around by way of the railway to the foot of the climb a mile beyond Rogers Pass station took an hour and a half and then the fun began. There we left the last semblance of trail and crossed the creek with the help of an improvised plank drawbridge.
The climb up through the burnt timber was exasperatingly hard because the luxuriant undergrowth concealed the rough ground and every stumble and fall involved a thorough sprinkling from the rain-wet bush. We had had one hard shower, while en route from the Glacier House to Rogers Pass,—but by six o'clock, when we had reached a charming spot, 'way up in the timbers, for camp, the clouds had lifted and the night cleared off. The small tent was soon pitched and a rousing fire going. We dried off while supper was in preparation and eating, and enjoyed a magnificent, fine view off to the S.S.W.—Mount Bonney I believe—and Mount Macdonald rose high above our heads to the left or east. When we turned

in at 9 o'clock my pack thermometer showed 48 degrees F. I slept well and was perfectly comfortable without even a blanket. At 1.30 I woke up and found the night temperature just the same outside—and 54 degrees F. in the tent. After knocking the fire together and adding more wood, I turned in again till 3 a.m. when I got up to watch the day dawn. Somewhere about 4.30, while we were finishing breakfast, the sun came up—behind the clouds from us—but where it threw the most exquisite rose pink light on the snow capped peaks off to the south. Truly, the few minutes during which that sight lasts are worth almost any amount of climbing and discomforts to see. We left camp by quarter of five and prayed for the clouds to lift. They didn't. In a half hour the rain came down in such a determined, businesslike sort of way there was nothing left to do but to return to the tent and wait awhile to see if it would not clear off in the early forenoon in time for us to continue. We four crowded back again under cover and tried to while away the time by singing, S. and myself —Edward and his son contented themselves with the applause and audience part, no amount of joshing would move them to sing. We sang and told stories till we were tired and then discovered Edward and son were peacefully snoring. Then we went to sleep and snored. When we woke up at eight o'clock the rain was still coming straight down so we tried to compose a poem to commemorate our exploits. After much striving and strenuous assistance the poet wrought, most painfully, the following verse—

From Glacier four men went out to explore
Determined the top of Mount Tupper to soar
But the rain from on high
Came down by and by
So they lay in their tent and did snore.—Evermore

J. H. Batcheller

Sir James Hector and Edward Whymper. Photo by Mary Schäffer.

Sir James Hector

Sir James Hector, geologist, botanist, & surveyor, for the Palliser Expedition, which explored the mountains & rivers lying between Laggan & Golden during the years '57 to '60, returned to Canada for the first time in Aug. of 1903 accompanied by his younger son Douglas, a young man of brilliant mind & great promise. They reached Glacier on Aug. 12th, where the son showed symptoms of serious illness, & was removed to Revelstoke Hospital. There he died, & on Aug. 17th his body was laid to rest. Within sound of the river his father had explored so many years ago, & in the shadow of the mountains where his best manhood had been spent; the son lies today.

The father, his heart too heavy to continue his journey, or to carry out his plans, that night turned his face westward and returned to New Zealand by the vessel which had borne both to the Canadian shore. Though so short a time among us, yet in that time his genial hearty manner, his delightful conversation in the old exploring days made all who came in contact with him his friends.

The accompanying pictures were taken the afternoon he started on his return trip. Mr. Edw. Whymper, the famous climber, & Sir James Hector the most famous Canadian Rocky Mt. Explorer, met for the first time that day, but the handclasp was one of a long established friendship.

Mrs. Chas. Schäffer*

**Mary Schäffer Warren (1861-1939), a Philadelphian, first came to the mountains in 1889 as a friend of Mary Vaux. Continuing the work of her first husband, Dr. Charles Schäffer, she produced* Alpine Flora of the Canadian Rockies *with Stewardson Brown. She made extensive wilderness trips to the headwaters of the North Saskatchewan and Athabasca Rivers and in 1908 became the first person to extensively explore the Maligne Lake area in Jasper National Park. It was at this time she named Mount Mary Vaux. She published* Old Indian Trails of the Canadian Rockies, *an account of these journeys, in 1911.*

Mount Abbott on Snowshoes.

On Wednesday the Third of February 1904, with Edward Feuz, jr. as guide, I essayed a mountain climb. It was midwinter and an unfathomed quantity of snow covered valleys and mountains. The snow pack in the Selkirks is always great, and the snow lies loose and heavy except where wind and sun have good opportunity. Feb. 3rd 1904 was overcast, the sun seldom showed itself, and snow fell,though lightly, all through the day.

We left Glacier at 5:25, put on snowshoes, and immediately plunged into the heavy timber on the lower slopes of Mt. Abbott. There was no sign of the summer trail and we made our own track. We left Marion Lake to our right as we climbed. The way was steep for snowshoes but we gave ourselves time in the most trying places. At 8 o'clock we passed two trees bearing blaze-marks, probably marking a path to the side of the mountain facing Glacier Crest and the Asulkan Glacier. At 9:30 we were at the timberline. We decided to make a long detour to the right to some more gentle slopes for the ascent of the ridge. At 10 we began the steep part of our work. We had to be very careful rounding the side facing Ross Peak, and for a time were directly under an overhanging cornice of snow. By 11:35 we were past the worst, and found it pleasant work on the long slope of snow which reaches upward to the peak. Here the snow was harder and bore up our snowshoes well. Soon we were on the crest, and as long-distance views were shut off by the falling snowflakes, contented ourselves with local views, the most significant of which were the overhanging cornices. And we got into closer relation with what a cornice may mean than we had expected or intended. The slopes being steep at one portion of the crest, we kept well up on the crest itself. I learned the lesson that it is not simply the actual overhang that may fall, but that the break-off may take a slice out of the snowbank itself as well. When we reached the rocks that led right up to the peak, we found them covered with tightly-packed snow, so taking off our snowshoes which were inadequate for the final 50 ft. or so, we clambered up to the cairn or stone man with the flag frozen round the little pole. It was now 12:10 and bitterly cold. Provisions were frozen and our gloves and mitts were so icy that it was hard to get a hold upon our ice-axes and alpenstocks. We had taken both these implements for surer work with our snowshoes. I left a little memorandum book with a few lines as to our itinerary, placing it in a niche between 2 stones— but it was so cold with gloves off I could hardly write. We took a hasty lunch and started down at 12:30. We followed on our tracks for a good way and had to be cautious getting round the steep slope that had lost so much time for us on the ascent. This place needed some balancing, and cautious slow progressing, but we did not rope as we had done on coming up. At 2:10 we were at the timber line. It had taken 4 hrs. to climb up to this height from Glacier House, but, thanks mainly to opportunities for snowshoe glissades, we came down in exactly one hour, reaching the hospitable hotel at ten minutes after three.

The record of this trip may serve to show that something can be done, even in mid winter and on snowshoes, in the matter of mountain climbing. With special adaptations, such as changing from snowshoes to boots in dangerous places, there might even be some advantages in winter climbing. Ed Feuz jr. made a splendid guide & companion.

J. C. Herdman*

**The Reverend J.C. Herdman (1856-1910) was the pastor of Knox Presbyterian Church in Calgary from circa 1890 until his death in 1910. He was a founding member of the Alpine Club of Canada and made several first ascents in the Rockies and Selkirk Mountains. In addition to his mountaineering achievements, he was one of the first recreational snowshoers in the mountains and completed a number of major winter outings along the CPR line.*

June 6, 1904

A delightful summer resort. We arrived on the afternoon of the 6th, well after five; and beginning an hour after our arrival it rained and snowed fairly continuously till our departure on 7 June. The principal event was going to and from the dining room fully exposed to the weather. The Lady Superintendent was most kind and agreeable and deserves the Albert Medal for helping all alike under a trying and depressing environment.

L. & H. Geary

A Novice on Cheops
August 24, 1904

"Only two persons have been known to climb that mountain," and my informant turned away with a shrug of his shoulders. What better incentive could a youngster have to try it? My previous experience of climbing had been to climb Eagle Peak on the day before, of which my chief memories were bruised shins and sore fingers, smoke from forest fires having spoiled the view usually obtainable; this, and climbing Observatory Hill in Greenwich Park comprised my experience of this fascinating pastime. The pyramid of rock which forms the summit of Cheops had an attraction for me that I seemed incapable of resisting. Stiff? Yes, I was rather but that I thought would soon wear off. It was 9:30 on Saturday morning when I saluted the grave & sedate guide Christian Bohren (who seems to have his full share of the "Peace of the Mountains") with "Will you take me up Cheops today, Bohren?" He opened his eyes and ejaculated "Why? Sure!" In ten minutes we were off up the track in the direction of Rogers Pass at a gait which evidently meant business. At the eastern end of No. 14 shed (about two miles from Glacier House) we struck into the bush & made good time for nearly five minutes; then my troubles began, even Scotch knitted stockings will not stay in position when various thorns, broken boughs, are doing their best at every step to pull them off; here my guide, who seemed to be prepared for all emergencies, produced a pair of puttees from the depths of his pack and proceeded to bind my stockings on in a way which defied both bush & rock. Have you ever tried scrambling & climbing through clumps of stout bushes and bunches of raspberry canes, tripping over dead branches and stepping into mud holes? If not, I would make bold to suggest that you try, say, a few hundred yards, with no particular object in view. . . . My pacemaker was sauntering along with an easy swing, logs and rocks apparently not disturbing his equanimity in the slightest degree, while the perspiration was dropping from me in a way that promised to run me dry in a very short time. About halfway through this tangled mass I had the pleasure (?) of adding a, to me, new experience to my list in the shape of the enmity of a tribe of wasps. I wonder what I did to cause such a commotion, or did they consider that I was getting too far behind my guide and proceed to hasten me as much as they could? However that may be, they commenced operations on a scale that caused me to bolt over logs and through bushes as if I were mad. What is a wasp sting like? I should think that red-hot pins applied to one's face and neck would give some idea. With a yell I made off after Christian who looked at me with surprise written all over his countenance, apparently thinking I had gone mad. By this time, I had killed about a dozen of the attacking force and the remainder retired in good order evidently considering that they had done their duty and driven me from their castle. Mopping my face, I excitedly exclaimed "Wasps!" to which the man, whom I had bought for the day, leisurely replied "Vaspen? Y-e-e-s, vaspen vairee-bad-dis-yeer."
He is a cool man is Christian Bohren, his English is certainly weak, but he had my life hanging at the end of his rope several times that day and I should not hesitate to trust it there again; nothing in the shape of a precipice or wall of ice or snow seemed to disturb him in the least. He will stand and chop holes in the ice at the top of a 500 ft. precipice with nothing but a few inches of ice between him and the next life, looking as if it were nothing at all out of the ordinary and a novice at the end of his ropes liable to slip and give him a send-off through the Styx at any minute. I used to think that these men earned their money easily, but I had changed my mind entirely; however, I am drifting from my story and must get back to the bush. We soon reached a creek bed which ran up to the first bench and I was very glad to get my feet onto the rocks and do an hour up this irregular stairway; there were loose rocks and I got all wet, but what did that matter? It was far preferable to wasps, fallen trees etc. etc.? At the top of this creek we reached a small plain strewn with boulders and sparsely covered with grass; here, my guide informed me, goats grazed; at least I presume that was what he meant when he pointed to the grass and said "Goats!" It was hot, and Christian Bohren reminded me of the motto I had often seen on a furniture mover's van at home, short and concise but very full of meaning, namely "I keep moving." At this point we rested for fully four or five minutes & then started off for that pyramid which looked further off than it had done an hour and a half before. We walked up for a few hundred feet on a nice hard bed of snow and then got onto a stretch of loose rock that must have had a very trying effect on my temper if it had not been for the absolute serenity of that guide; rocks did not seem to turn over under his feet, snow did

not let him through and the heat seemed to suit him admirably; in this way we proceeded for about half an hour when suddenly I heard a slight rumbling and my guide, shouting "rocks," did a sprint for a hundred yards that would have done credit to a mountain goat, I followed at a more clumsy gait but kept out of the track of those rocks which thundered down like a waterfall in spring. Bohren just glanced up as if he had been dodging rocks all his life and said "this way," pointing to a mass of solid rock and snow that bordered the rock slide which we negotiated in about an hour of solid climbing and then reached a small snow field which ended with a solid wall of ice and frozen snow that seemed to me to effectually bar all further progress. We were nearly at the base of the pyramid and our position I will try to describe as well as I can remember it: we had reached what might roughly be described as the apex of a triangular field of snow, to our right a few rocks edged a precipice which, on enquiry my guide informed me, was about 500 ft. deep and a sheer drop too, which would not have troubled us had we slipped over; a few yards higher up we walked along a ridge of snow, with this accommodating precipice on one side and a fissure in the glacier on the other, which ridge widened out to meet the before-mentioned wall of ice; I planted my feet firmly in the snow and stuck my ice axe in as far as possible and said to myself for the second or third time "Well, you are an a idiot." I looked at my guide who appeared to be sizing me up and who greeted my look with the cool remark "preety steep," to which I replied "yes, a bit," feigning an unconcern which I did not feel. He had not been up Cheops before, and if he had suggested giving it up, I would have easily forgiven him but it apparently did not enter his mind; taking his axe, he proceeded to cut steps in the wall which had a decidedly outward slope and would have puzzled a cat; two steps convinced him that even he could not hope to succeed in tackling it at that spot so he gave it up, and after a few minutes search he found a place about twenty feet high with a suspicion of a slope in our favor and, to a green hand like myself, about as good to climb as the wall of a jerry-built house; here Christian commenced to cut holes for our feet and went up step by step with the writer following. We must have looked like flies on a wall. Strange to say it did not feel at all doubtful as to our safety although the least slip as far as I could see would have shot us down that precipice in double quick time. I only saw the humourous side of it. I looked like a criminal going to execution with a rope round my neck, pieces of ice that my guide was cutting kept running down my back in a stream that would have cooled the hottest fire-eater on record. At last we reached the top of that wall, the guide keeping a strain on the rope all the way. The next little trouble was a wall of solid rock which formed one side of the base of the pyramid; I had by now such faith in the powers of my guide that I half-expected to see him swarm up that, but he did not try it. A glance showed him a ledge of rock about three or four inches wide which ran round one corner of the pyramid and away he went, I following the end of that rope, feeling that it was no worse than the snow wall; round this corner we got on to a mass of loose rock through which we climbed to the top where my guide astonished me by giving vent to a shout and I selected a soft rock to lie on in the sun and demolish my share of the fruit in our luncheon bag. The summit commands a splendid view of the local scenery, but long distance views were spoiled by the smoke from forest fires which covered the country with an atmosphere as dense as that of London. We stayed on the summit for 3/4 of an hour; it seemed to me like fifteen minutes; we had taken four hours and thirty minutes to ascend the northerly face and descended the side facing Ross Peak in two hours and thirty minutes to the railway track at Ross Peak water tank. Another hour saw us at Glacier House which I was truly thankful to reach, my feet sore and my body aching all over, but Christian Bohren looked good for the same trip over again. I am now trying to solve the question as to why people (myself in particular) climb mountains.

W. W. Le Feaux
Revelstoke, British Columbia & London, England

Mt. Bonney
First Ascent by a Lady
Friday, Sept. 2, 1904

On Sept. 1st I chanced to be seated comfortably on Mt. Afton with Christian Bohren, from where Mt. Bonney looked so superlatively beautiful that then and there we decided to "try it" next day. Wherefore by 3:15 a.m. on the 2nd Sept. Bohren and I were astride sure-footed cayuses & on these we made our way to the second bench on Mt. Abbott. The moon had paled & the stars had fled before the first rays of the sun, when at 5:15, we parted from our steeds & their guide.

We started at a steady pace to the right passing a patch of snow which bore the footprints of some huge bear. Soon we had turned the shoulder of Abbott & Mt. Bonney came into view, a steady scramble over boulders brought us to the valley between Abbott & Afton, more scrambling over large boulders varied by struggles through scrub pine & rhododendron and we reached the first moraine of the Lily Glacier. The foot of the Lily was crossed, then its second moraine and by 8 o'clock we were by the foot of Bonney's huge fissured glacier.

Now we had to decide our route, for Ch. Bohren had never been on Mt. Bonney before, moreover very few ascents had ever been made; we were far to the left of the glacier, and in front of us, afar off, there was a saddle, steep snow & a small amount of rock appeared to lead to it. To the right for a great distance the rocks were perpendicular, we decided to go for the saddle. Many detours had to be made to avoid the crevasses and there was much step cutting. At length we reached the base of the mountain and work began in earnest, up a long steep ice & snow field we scrambled & reached the bad piece of rock we had seen from below; here Bohren was prospecting for some feasible way upwards when an avalanche pounded down the slope we had just left. Snow did not seem so interesting for a little while. With some difficulty we found a way over the bad bit of rock, and eventually reached the snow-wall & cornice at the top. It was 10:30, half an hour after we made our first halt and had some welcomed breakfast. The views were magnificent: to the south stretched a vast snow-field; then over the Geikie snow-field we saw Dawson, Deville & Fox with many other magnificent peaks, most of them as yet nameless & unscaled. Sir Donald & the adjacent peaks were to the eastward over the peaks on the Asulkan; to the west lay the steep snow-fields which we had yet to cross to reach the summits. After half an hour we started & made the first point on which is a cairn presumably erected by Mr. Wheeler—a long descent & very steep snow-field brought us to the next summit on which we built a stone-man and we immediately started for the third point a considerable distance off but of about the same altitude. Here there was a cairn & this was the summit made by Mr. Green in '88 when he had made the first ascent of Mt. Bonney. We reached this summit at 1 o'clock. We then proceeded down an easy snow slope for 1/2 an hour & made a second short halt. By two o'clock we began the descent. We had decided not to return over the various points & considered the distance to the moraines of Ross Peak too great, though this would probably have been the best way. The slope we had chosen soon turned into wet shale devoid of footholds, & this in turn gave place to an excessively steep ice field wherein ladder-like steps were cut with much difficulty, after two extremely unpleasant hours we reached the glacier by four o'clock, were off it by five and started home across the shoulder of Afton & Abbott. This homeward scramble became somewhat severe after dark and it was ten o'clock before we reached Glacier House—we had been nineteen hours out—Christian Bohren's skill and patience were beyond praise.

Henrietta L. Tuzo*
Warlingham, England

Mount Bonney and the Lily Glacier from Mount Abbott, July 26, 1897.

Sept. 5, 1904

Ascent of Avalanche Crest by the undersigned—a little girl of 6 years & 7 months.

Eleanor Carrole Robbins

**Henrietta Loetitia Tuzo Wilson (1873-1955) was born in Victoria, the daughter of one of British Columbia's pioneer doctors who came west with the Hudson's Bay Company fur brigades in 1853. She was educated in England. An original member of the Alpine Club of Canada, she attended the club's first camp in 1906. She is noted for completing a number of ascents in the Rockies and Selkirks which were more difficult than those being attempted by the average lady alpinist of her day. Together with her guide, Christian Kaufmann, she made the first ascent of the seventh peak in the Valley of the Ten Peaks which today bears her maiden name—Mount Tuzo.*

Oct. 11, 1904

Are you broken down by your business, are you disgusted with the life; are you fighting with your family or your relatives, are you hunting for a charming place to isolate your sorrows or your troubles.
Don't hesitate, go straight to Glacier House—remain there one long week and after you will be in the finest condition to meet the awful life again.

I. Garnier de L'Estoille
France

July 20, 1905

Ascent of Mt. Sifton 9,061 ft.—F. Meinecke Jr. with guide Ed. Feuz Jr.

There was much conversation about the high peaks and beautiful mountain scenery of the Selkirks all last winter at our home and I took great interest as I am very fond of hunting and out-of-door sports. I was highly delighted when I was asked to join my father's party to the mountains and had made up my mind to scale Sir Donald. However, here I met with trouble. I was told a boy of 17 years had not enough experience in life to use the proper judgement and care, which are necessary for reaching the very high and dangerous pinnacles, in other words I was set way back. But, showing that I was careful in other climbs, I finally secured the consent of my father to scale Mt. Sifton and I can see that it was a hard task rewarded by a view which I shall never forget. The experience of going up to the Hermit Chalet, sleeping there, cooking our own meals was good fun. Going up to the top at 6 a.m. was a hard climb, but sliding down some of the steep parts was a great sensation.

Ferd. Meinecke, Jr.

Aug. 7th, 1905

Avalanche, 9365 ft., is a high and hard enough mountain to scale for anyone who does not claim to be an especially skillful climber. A very thirsty pony took me a little beyond the Summit Cascade, and at 8.10 a.m. Edouard Feuz Jr. and I commenced our day's work. We did the moraine slowly and comfortably, and roped up on having reached the first glacier. Soon a thrilling incident happened. Edouard lost his pipe, which came sliding towards me but was promptly stopped in its wild and mad careen down the glacier. The loss of this comforter would have been a serious blow to Edouard, and might have spoiled his temper and our trip. A wide crevasse across the glacier—a part of the actual bergschrund—presented a wonderful, awe-inspiring sight. Edouard pronounced it more like a thousand ft. deep—we could not see the bottom of it—and huge icicles which had formed in it adorned its walls like so many gigantic prisms. Once across the bergschrund, the ascent was soon accomplished and we reached the summit at 10.00 a.m.—not a bit tired. The weather was ideal, the view of the Selkirks perfect but the Rockies hidden, owing to smoke. I tried to count the glaciers and snow peaks which were ever increasing in number as we approached the summit, but found it an impossible task; suffice it to say that the sight of that still, white world of eternal snow and sublime grandeur can never be forgotten by one who has been fortunate enough to behold it. We encountered again some difficulty in crossing the bergschrund on our way down, but Edouard proved himself master of the situation and had no pity on me when I declared myself unable to cross the schrund where he wanted me to. I simply had to do it and accomplished the seemingly impossible feat quite easily after all. Now followed two most exhilarating glissades, and then the walk across the glacier, or rather snowfield, to Avalanche Crest. Here we unroped and our homeward journey began in earnest. A brood of ptarmigan bade us welcome on our return into the world of the living, and the little things were so ignorant of fear and the wiles of men, we could have caught them on the spot. We reached the hotel a few minutes to seven, after a 12 hours' most enjoyable outing. The view from Avalanche amply compensates for "that tired feeling" which the excursionist will experience upon his return, and Edouard Feuz Jr. cannot be improved upon as a guide.

Lulu Grau
Honolulu, Hawaiian Islands

Guides chopping steps, 1903.

August, 1905 The surroundings here might easily inspire one to write poetry, but I am unable to find anything to rhyme with "Illecillewaet."

G. A. Cavendish
Boulder, Mont. U.S.A.

August 13, 1905 Ladies! Be sure and bring your riding skirts with you. The men here are bashful. Pooh!

[Anon]

August, 1905 Have been here for four days & though I have done no climbing—except Eagle Peak which calls for no comment—am satisfied that this could be made one of the ten best, as well as one of the most beautiful, climbing centres in the world. But a sufficiency of guides is essential: six or eight really good guides, anxious & willing to do difficult work, together with a few "porters" or junior guides to take ladies & non-climbers on to the glacier, over the Asulkan Pass to Avalanche Crest etc., is the very least number with which anything could be done. The present system of paying guides is also unsatisfactory. They should be paid direct by the climber & each climb should have its price proportioned to the difficulty of the ascent as in Switzerland. At present there is no real inducement to the guide to choose the good climbs, or indeed to climb at all, & there are so many competing for them, that they tend to become both lazy & unduly filled with a sense of their own importance. A few more trails would be desirable, & I would strongly urge the building of a chalet or small hotel on the ledge of Mt. Abbott, which would take the place the old Riffelberg did at Zermatt, & enable those who can't walk much to enjoy the magnificent panorama from Mt. Abbott & form a convenient starting point for climbing.

L. S. Amery* A. C.
London, England

**The Rt. Hon. Leopold Stennett Amery (1873-1955) was one of Great Britain's most noted statesmen during the first half of the 20th century. He sat for 34 years in the House of Commons and held a number of important ministerial portfolios in various Conservative governments. An avid mountaineer, he climbed extensively around the world and served as president of the Alpine Club. Amery made a number of visits to Canada in his lifetime and, beginning with his first trip in 1905, climbed in the Rockies on nearly every occasion. In 1909 he was a member of a party which made one of the earliest attempts to climb Mount Robson, and in 1929 he made the first ascent of the mountain on the North Saskatchewan River which bears his name.*

Aug. 19, 1905 Mt. Abbott by a lady in an afternoon.

A little stroll up to Marion Lake, made for exercise on a rainy afternoon developed quite unpremeditatively into a delightful ascent of Abbott Peak, which is here recorded to encourage any good walker with some experience on steep slopes to try the same.

Starting at 1.45, Miss P. F. Morris of Philadelphia and the writer left Glacier House in the characteristic *rainy* weather of this place, and reached Marion Lake in something less than an hour. Ignoring adverse conditions and led on by the hope of a change, we pressed on in clouds and rain over the amphitheatre at treeline (marked by numerous stone-men) and scrambled up the steep slopes to the ridge, which was reached about 4. To our delight, the weather then suddenly changed and the clouds broke away, revealing a most wonderful view on all sides. After a halt of 15 minutes, we passed along the mile or so of arête with speed, and arrived at the summit of Mt. Abbott at 5.05, Mt. Afton towering above us very near and temptingly. Lack of time prevented thoughts of its ascent, however. The view of the Sir Donald, Dawson, Bonney & Swiss groups of peaks was magnificent.

Return was made the same way, starting at 5.20, & Glacier House was reached at 7.10, the descent from Marion Lake being made in 18 minutes. The whole trip was made in quick time for a lady.

A phenomenon worth noting occurred on the ridge: After the breaking up of the worst clouds, the sun shone clearly on the western side of the arête, while for a ½ hour the mists continued thick on the east side. Our shadows were cast very distinctly on the mists; around these were perfect rainbow shadows in circles like halos—a most extraordinary mist effect.

J. H. Scattergood
Philadelphia

Sept. 7, 1905

I should like to point out to American & Canadian visitors to this place that the word Glacier is not pronounced Glazier as most of them think. ("Glac" as in Lass.) A glazier I may remind them is one who fixes window panes.

R. M. G.

Omnibuses at Glacier!
July 12, 1906

Upon the arrival of one of the Westbound trains, an English lady hopped off, rushed up to one of the guests of the Glacier House Hotel and delivered the following query: "I beg your pardon, but will you be so kind as to tell me where I may find an omnibus to drive me up to the Glacier?" To anyone who has been there, a chart or diagram of the foregoing will be absolutely superfluous.

J. H. Goodwin
of 1215 Broadway, New York

The Caves of Cheops
(Deutschman Caves)
July 22, 1906

To the many guests at Glacier House who consider a visit to the Deutschman Caves in the Cougar Valley it may be that the following brief description of what is involved in the trip will be of interest.

As is mostly the case in this region the distance from Glacier House has been variously estimated at from 9 to 11 miles. In time about 2½ hours should be allowed for the trip one way, and of course this will vary with the condition of the trail and the desire of the visitors to stay and enjoy the superb views which form a continuous panorama from start to finish. With a prompt start at 7 o'clock there will be ample time to form a very correct idea of the caves, and to return in time for late dinner the same evening.

At the time of our visit we went first about 1½ miles up the valley [past the main camp] to a point where at one time a pretty lake had existed, but is now only a flat owing to the breaking of the moraine dam. From the slopes at this point beautiful views looking back may be had of Mt. Sir Donald & the Illecillewaet Glacier. Returning and going down the valley we suddenly came out upon a narrow point of rock and our guide informed us we were standing upon the edge of Old Point Comfort. On one side we looked down a dizzy height of several hundred feet and we realized that the spot where we stood jutted out over this chasm some 20 feet. On the way back to the caves we noted a point from which this jutting rock could be seen in sharp profile against the sky, with Mt. Sir Donald and the glacier in the distance far below it. It made a striking photograph with Mr. Deutschman posed in an easy position on the very edge.

Charles Deutschman standing on Old Point Comfort, Illecillewaet Glacier in background, 1906.

But our main object, the exploration of the caves, was still before us, and armed with candles and acetylene lamps we prepared to descend the upper one, known as "The Natural Bridge." These caves have been formed by the stream from the upper valley which passes the several underground passages and has worn out of the solid rock a series of potholes and caverns. The entire stream suddenly disappears from view into a yawning hole only to reappear again several hundred feet further down the valley. Here it has worn for itself a deep narrow channel through which it whirls like a millrace. A few hundred feet below it again plunges into a large opening, the surfaces of which are worn into smooth potholes by the constant action of the water, dashing with a loud roar and throwing the spray high in the air. A little below is an opening into the underground passage by which one may look down and discern the foam of the water as it rushes along and disappears from view only to come to light again for a few feet at the bottom of a great lake said to be 85 feet deep, and then to pass from view finally.

Visitors may pass into these caves by 3 points, the first or upper one being by a lateral branch some 80 feet from the stream. One passes down a long, narrow way, the ceiling of which becomes lower and lower until a tall man must stoop low. The air is not cold, but very still, and the roar of water on ahead may be heard. A ladder carries one down 10 feet, and the stream is rushing at one side, emerging from a great vaulted hole, and tearing by, disappearing beyond. Partly crawling, partly walking, the stream may be followed down a considerable distance on a ledge to the right which rises and falls, sometimes being level with the water edge, and again 18 or 20 feet above it. There is no stalactite formation but the rock everywhere shows the result of water erosion against the strata of different hardnesses, some of the plates of rock being worn thin almost as paper, and yet solid and firm as ever. A piece of magnesium wire reveals the roof above, now vaulted, now covered with thick, hard plates of rock, flat as flag pavement, and now and then a dark passage leading off into some unknown depths of darkness. A crystal drop on every projection of rock catches and reflects the light of the torch, the smoke from which drifts lazily along making a weird indistinctness to the whole scene.

The entrance to the second cave—which is really known as No. 1—is found just below the point where the water emerges from the Natural Bridge, and is entirely dry, the stream for the present having chosen to flow above the ground through the millrace & descend by another opening. A set of stone steps, formed by nature, assisted by man, leads down out of the sunlight and into a great pothole. This opens into another of almost equal size, the bottom of which is perhaps 10 feet lower and is reached by a ladder, rough but strong and with the rungs at least 2 feet apart. Pothole after pothole is passed, some dry, some with a little water in the bottom, and others with water over one's head, but the height and breadth ever increasing, and the roar of water always ahead. There are several turns and one emerges into a great amphitheatre across one end of which the stream, just out of the light and air above, has worn for itself a broad bed, and the whole is dimly lighted by some stray rays struggling in between the waves of spray. The shelving rocks are covered with masses of ice not yet melted after the winter's cold and these and the water drops on the dripping rocks reflect every flash of the lantern or magnesium wire.

To one of a daring temperament the descent of 85 feet on the end of a rope to the bottom of the cañon may offer some attraction, but it should only be attempted by those with steady heads and a familiarity with such work. Our party voted such experiences were not for us, but Mr. Deutschman* gave us a description of the labyrinth of passages, the immense chambers with stalactites, and the great rock, flat as a floor and having an area of 1200 square feet.

And now just a word as to the formation of these natural wonders. Ages ago some convulsion of nature formed a great crack in the earth which time filled with limestone rock. The stream in turn began to wear this softer stone away, the results of ages amounting to the potholes and caverns we see today. A fault in the crack left a roof of harder rock, and changes in the inlets making some of the caverns dry and some the bed of the stream.

In conclusion the trip to the Caves is well worth the exertion, the trail is excellent and safe and the views superb. To anyone who is able to descend a ladder the visit to the Caves is perfectly safe, and under the guidance of Mr. Deutschman will be of great interest and lasting memory.

William S. Vaux
Philadelphia, Penna. (American Alpine Club, Alpine Club of Canada)

**Charles Henry Deutschman was a trapper who discovered the Nakimu Caves in the Cougar Valley, approximately four miles west of Glacier House, in 1904. He staked mineral claims to the property which he subsequently sold to the Dominion Government. Deutschman was hired as caretaker of the caves in 1905 and later served as a forest officer in Glacier Park. He eventually resigned his position in 1918, in part due to his frustration with the lack of development and parks department support at the caves. A steady deterioration in the facilities at the caves as well as walkways and ladders inside caused the parks department to close them to the public in 1929.*

Sept., 1906 A fable for authors. Once upon a time an American Lady came to Glacier and not only visited the Glacier itself, but also met a gentleman whom she called a Little Englander, because the area of his mind was scarcely as big even as the little island he came from. Knowing his kind, she asked him with a spirit to be envied and with due solemnity whether the C.P.R. had put the Glacier there as an advertisement. Solemnly he treasured the sample of the intelligence of ladies from the States, and when with a friend he wrote his little book he solemnly printed the story on page 222. And the American Lady has often told it all with glee to her American friends. *Moral:* When Little Englanders travel here, they should be accompanied by some one from the "States" to point out to them what is a joke, and what is not a joke.

U.S.A.

Sir Donald
July 26, 1907 First ascent of the year.

Party Miss Jean Parker. Winnipeg
Frank W. Freeborn New York
Eduoard Feuz, Sr.
" " Jr.

Timetable 4.00 leave hotel
6.00 reach glacier
7.45 cross bergschrund and begin cliff climbing
8.30 finish skirting head-wall
9.30 cross rock-infested couloir
11.55 reach summit
12.35 leave "
5.35 cross bergschrund
6.15 leave glacier for moraine
7.40 reach hotel

Weather All sorts—sunshine, clouds, mist, snow squall, hail, sleet, rain, alternating and mixed

Views Fine first half of way up, superb nearly all the way down. The views of the Illecillewaet Névé, the Asulkan Glacier, the peaks and icefields from the north around by the west and south nearly to the east were indescribably proud and picturesque.

Snow slopes The rock debris and the glacier from the lower moraine to the head wall were so covered with deep snow that we could use the slope as a stairway going up and a slide coming down.

Difficulties The two most notable difficulties of recent years, the wide bergschrund and the falling rocks, were absent. The late snows had made an excellent bridge over the bergschrund, and from some cause not seen not a rock fell in the dreaded couloir while we were in or near it. I must differ with my friend, Prof. H. C. Parker, who says, "The climbing from the couloir to the summit was of the most elementary and easy description." With his exceptional experience in difficult climbs his depreciating of the difficulties may be natural; but for nine-tenths of those who are likely to make the ascent the difficulties and dangers of the rocks and cliffs are real, and great skill and caution are needed all the way from the bergschrund to the summit. The fact that we were forty minutes longer in the descent of that portion than in the ascent sufficiently shows the character of the work. A novice in climbing or a person not physically fortified by recent climbing should not attempt Sir Donald.

Frank W. Freeborn.*
New York

Mary J. Vaux, William S. Vaux Jr., and Mary M. Vaux. *ca* 1907.

August 12, 1907 I highly endorse the grandeur of these mountains. Dee-Lighted! I approve of them.

T. Rose. Velt

P.S. I am sure the Almighty will feel relieved.

W. E.

**Frank W. Freeborn (1847-1919) taught Latin in high schools in Boston, Massachusetts and Brooklyn, New York. An avid alpinist and photographer, he travelled extensively in Europe before first coming to Glacier House in 1905. A founding member of the Alpine Club of Canada in 1906, he returned to the mountains to participate in all of the annual camps until ill health incapacitated him in 1914.*

Asulkan Pass
Aug. 19th, 1907

This ascent, which most climbers would consider a mere "bagatelly" under ordinary conditions, was done by us today after what we are told was one of the longest spells of wet weather known in the mountains.

We left the hotel at 8:30 A.M. on what were supposed to be sure-footed ponies but one of our party had to dismount after going less than one quarter of the way into the Asulkan Valley due to his horse's stumbling at least a dozen times & going down on his knees no less than four times. As the boggy trail is very narrow in parts & high above the river, we advise the utmost care in selection of horses as you are apt to be given any old thing they have on hand.

The snow on the glacier started about three inches deep but before we had proceeded very far we were in up to our knees & this arduous work continued all the way to the top of the pass—in several places our alpenstocks going into the snow to their full length. The summit was not reached until 1:45 P.M. The view is simply superb & we cannot too highly recommend this climb when conditions are favorable. Ed. Feuz Sr. is a most capable & obliging guide & it was a great coincidence to meet him in this distant place—so far from our mutual stomping ground, Grindelwald & Lauterbrunnen.

In justice to the genial & courteous manager of this excellent hotel we add that the horses are not run in connection with it.

Robert St. Mainzer
Jola Powell Mainzer
New York City

(who probably wore the first patent leather low shoes & white vest seen on the Pass!!) Ed. C. Steidrich Jr.
Peoria, Ill.

George Vaux Sr. (2nd from left), Mary J. Vaux (on right) and her husband George Vaux Jr. (standing), 1907.

Sept. 30–Oct 2, 1907

Am well acquainted with the Swiss Alps, Engadine, Tyrol, and Norway, their glaciers & scenery—& only wonder that some of those who frequent those wonders of nature, do not in greater numbers come to the Rockies. We'd gladly spend three weeks in this district instead of three days.

E. W. B. Trotter (Archdeacon)
Caracas, Venezuela, S.A.

July 6, 1908 Mt. Sir Donald 8 h. from Glacier (*alone*)

July 7, 1908 Asulkan Pass—Dawson Glacier

July 8, 1908 *Häsler Peak—Feuz Peak—Donkin Pass*: off Camp 1:15 a.m. Häsler P. 5:45. Feuz Peak 6:25. Michel Peak 9:00 a.m. Donkin Pass 12 a.m. Camp on Dawson F1. 1:15. Recommend the trip very much. (*made trip alone*)

July 9, 1908 Dawson G1.—Asulkan Pass—Glacier (5 h)

Eduord Franzelin C.E.
Gruneck, Tyrol, Austria

Card of Herr Franzelin found on Häsler Peak July 21, 1909 by E. W. D. Holway, H. Palmer, and F. K. Butters, time given thereon as above.

F. K. B.

July 17, 1908

Ho! Tourists bring your cameras,
The snapshots be this way.
The girls will ride in style astride
By Glacier House today.
The saddles that they ride in
Rise high both fore and aft,
And the wooden stirrups are the gems
Of saddlers' handicraft.
Let rain then drench the Selkirks
And blot out vale and hill,
The boys who've come from far abroad
Shall have some pictures still.
Gay is the chattering meal time,
The dancing hour is gay,
But the "willing" ride of the girls offside
Is the brightest hour of day.

The mountain smiles upon the brook,
The brook in answer purls,
And glaciers, hills, woods, birds and rills
Laugh at the jolly girls.
There's Illecillewaet the wag,
That naughty old névé,
He cracks his sides with Arctic glee,
His mirthful cheeks shed many a tear,
He "tips the wink" to "Donald" dear,
As the girls go by his way.
"Sir Donald" helios the news
Like wild fire 'round the peaks
To Hermit, Cougar 'cross the line,
To Uto and the Eagle crags,
To Dawson and the "Bonney" wags;
To see the girls in "breeks"
Gray-headed Dawson strains to look
Through the Asulkan Pass,
But the Hermit catches at a cloud
And says, "they're bold as brass."

When the longest meal is over
And the oldest pipe is lit,
When the most standoffish Johnny
Is thawing bit by bit,
When the mountaineers in circle
Up to the fireside creep,
And tell of crag and cornice
and ice crevasses deep,
When the Illecillewaet doth roar
From melting snow and rain,
When the great C.P.R. engines
Roar louder yet again,
When from the Chalet window
We watch the fountain play,
When the church bells on the engines
Recall the Sabbath day,
When the marmot sounds his whistle
And crouches on the stones,
When the red squirrel merrily
Gathers the hemlock cones,
When wails the wild mosquito
And drives his lancet in,
When all the guests with "Witch Hazel"
Are rubbing it well in,
With smiles and smothered laughter
Still is the story told
Of girls that ride in style astride
In saddles wet and cold.

[Tukiratu?]
Sydney, Australia

Julia Henshaw and Mary Schäffer on the trail to The Loop, 1910.

July 21, 1908

In a dash through the wonderful scenery of the CPR, over the Loop not exceeded in engineering in the world, for beauty and enjoyment, we halt at Glacier to be made at home by the genial host, and his gracious wife, in a perfect resting hostelry, which gives to the appetite a new vigor, and sends us on our way, travellers thoroughly rested and improved by the exhilarating air from the glacier, and the ever-attractive sight and music of the waterfall. Seeing many charming spots. We can offer nothing suggestive of improvement in management or delightful hospitality and kindness of its efficient heads.

Gen. Clay Goodlee U.S.M.C
& Bettie Goodlee
Washington City, D.C.

Sir Donald
August 8, 1908

The writer made the sixth ascent of this season in company with Edouard Feuz, Sr. The day was perfect and the conditions on the mountain the same.

Time: Left hotel 4 a. m. Reached glacier 6:00. Breakfast place on shelf above glacier 8:00. Summit 9:30. Descent: Left summit 10:30. Reached glacier 12:30. Left glacier 1:00. Hotel 2:00 in time for lunch.

Howard Palmer

August 16, 1908

The scenery and hotel here seem to be in good hands. Between God Almighty and the manager the traveller here gets more than his money's worth.

W. E. Guthrie
Bloomington, Ill.

June 3 & 4, 1909

We the undersigned are greatly indebted to the CPR for their generosity in delaying us at such a picturesque spot. We appreciate it very much, as it is a treat seldom afforded passengers who had not planned to stop off here. This was unavoidable, on account of the Land Slide, but we hope to stop here again on our return, from a trip around the world.

Katherine Gordon
Minneapolis, Minn.
Sydney B. Miller
Toronto, Ontario
Elisabeth E. Griffin
Syracuse, New York
R. H. Gale
Toronto, Ont.
[etc...]

July 26, 1909

I discovered on my first inspection today that the glacier once approached much nearer this House than at present. I regret that this practise has not been continued as the scramble over wet and rolling stones and the indiscriminate retreat through the rain are the only objections I have noted. 'As the Mt. did not come to the Mohammet—the alternative would have been to place the hotel nearer the glacier. Many other things I observed today, on my climb as far as the ice cave, but as they have mostly been already noted by the Messrs. Vaux, it will be unnecessary to make further mention. I should be pleased to make further observations, but as I leave tomorrow, I commit the task to others. This glacier is the culmination of a visit to the mts. which has been in all respects delightful—and enlightening.

Jos H. Winans
No. 7 Bevay, N.Y. City

May all "New Thought" people who pass this way stop and write a line to inspire others on their way.

G. B. W.
New York City, N.Y.

Mt. Avalanche
August 11, 1909

7:20 leave hotel
8:15 at foot of trail near Cascade summer house
9:20 in nearer end of crest
9:40 1st cairn
10:10 2d cairn
10:35 on upper edge of glacier, 20 minutes here for refreshments
10:55 rope up and move on
12:10 reach top of peak. Cloudy; picturesque but poor for photos.
3:10 leave top of peak
3:50 get on glacier
4:20 unrope at foot of glacier
5:10 at foot of trail
5:40 arrive at Glacier House
With Ernest Feuz, guide, whom I heartily recommend.

F. W. Freeborn
New York

A Third Trip beyond the Asulkan Pass
Aug. 1909

The two trips beyond the Asulkan Pass made during the summer of 1908 by Mssrs. E. W. D. Holway, Howard Palmer and F. K. Butters left in the minds of all three a desire to see more of that interesting region, and to penetrate further into its almost unknown valleys. Accordingly we met at the Glacier House July 11, 1909. We determined if possible to have some of our baggage packed for us across the first two ranges so we sent to Golden for a packer who had been previously on a trip to Mt. Sir Sandford with Mr. Palmer and others. The next day he arrived, and on the morning of July 13 we set off over the Asulkan Pass. We had our packs carried on ponies to the foot of the glacier. Before we had traversed half of the moraine the packer's burden proved too heavy for him and he divided it, carrying one half to the summit and then returning for the other part which he carried up and over the pass, leaving the first part near the summit. That evening we camped in the usual place above the Geikie Glacier, and the next morning set out to carry a relay up to the top of Donkin Pass. The packer meanwhile was to go back for the part of his pack left near the Asulkan Summit. That evening when we returned to camp he and his blankets had disappeared. Our half of our flour and sugar were on the top of Donkin Pass, the other half somewhere up the Asulkan—we supped on bacon, beans and tea, breakfasted on the same, and then went up the Asulkan after our abandoned stuff. We found it, and alongside was a stone with the scratched inscription "Gone back, the climb is too much for me." He was out four days' time and his fare from Golden to Glacier and return, but he evidently thought that it was a cheap escape. We were only delayed a day or two, and fortunately we were able to see the funny side of the affair. It was later reported to us at the Glacier House that he returned tired out. He had not done as much work in the two days as each of the other members of the party had done.

The next day we packed the rest of our outfit over Donkin Pass, and down to our campground of 1908 going back to the summit on the following afternoon for the remainder. That night there was a vicious hail and thunder storm and the next day it rained and snowed, giving us a good excuse for taking a much needed rest. Six days had been consumed in moving an outfit about fifteen miles, but we still had enough provisions for two weeks, and a most comfortable base camp.

Howard Palmer
Fred K. Butters
E. W. D. Holway*

**Edward W.D. Holway (1853-1923), Howard Palmer (1883-1944), and Frederic King Butters (1878-1945) were American mountaineers who climbed extensively in the Selkirk Mountains in the early 1900's. The trio did pioneering exploration in the northern end of the range from 1908 to 1912, and Palmer and Holway made the first ascent of the Northern Selkirks' most prominent peak, Mount Sir Sandford, in 1912. Palmer was a prominent member of both the Appalachian Mountain Club and the American Alpine Club and was the author of* Mountaineering and Exploration in the Selkirks *(1914). Both Holway and Butters were botanists from the University of Minnesota. Of all the contributors to the* Scrapbook *these gentlemen have suffered most in the editing. Their long detailed accounts of climbs and travels in the more remote areas of the Selkirks make fascinating reading, and they may yet appear in another publication.*

July 29, 1910 Was towed up Sir Donald by Edward Feuz. It is a wonderful experience for a novice—but accompanied by some shaking knees and occasional thoughts of an early funeral. The reward justifies the efforts and whatever danger (great or small according to the observer) there may be.

Dr. Laurence Selbing
Portland, Oregon

August 19, 1910

Say!
Isn't it great
The way the public
Expatiate
On climbs they make.
Why
All they do
Is sit and stew
And chat and chew
'Til the air is blue
About naught, too.
Well—
Wouldn't it bump you?
Sure.

[Anon]

August 20, 1910 Our first visit to this most glorious part of the country, opens our eyes indeed to the grandeur of the wonders of the works of God. As Americans & like most who think our wonders as those of far more magnificence than any others known, and believing our own "Rockies" to be unexcelled, we say & take off our hats to the "Selkirks" for our Rockies are only infants to these wonders —with which one will never tire—

Emil Bensbach
and Mrs. Emil Bensbach

August 25, 1910 Glacier deserves much praise. It is no doubt the prettiest place in the Rockies. Many thanks to the C.P.R. for opening up such a country of wonderful natural beauty. I have had many nice little jaunts and several good climbs while here. My leaving will be a reluctant one. Oh! Those lordly mountains reaching far up into the sky, covered here and there with snow and spotted with green foliage, and to the east the Great Glacier extremity a wondrous sight to see. Glacier will not be easily forgotten.

Richard Marat
Moose Jaw, Saskatchewan, Can.

Sept. 21, 1910 Having just returned from a much tiring but enjoyable walk to the "*Illegitimate* Glacier," can truly say it is the most beautiful and wonderful sight I have so far beheld and it makes me realize more fully than ever before how grand and beautiful the creations of God are and how thoughtful we should all be to the Creator of both Heaven and Earth . . .

Lenore E. Coffey
Columbus, Ohio

Group on CPR observation platform, 1910.

A Selected Bibliography:

Benjamin, Philip S. *The Philadelphia Quakers in the Industrial Age.* Philadelphia: Temple University Press, 1976.

Burpee, J. *Among the Canadian Alps.* New York: John Lane Co., 1914.

Cunningham, C. D. *The Pioneers of the Alps*, London: Sampson et al. 1888.

Doty, Robert. *Photo-Secession Stieglitz and the Fine-Art Movement in Photography.* New York: Dover Publications, 1978.

Gernsheim, Helmut and Alison. *The History of Photography.* New York: McGraw-Hill, 1969.

Hart, E. J. *A Hunter of Peace.* Banff; the Whyte Foundation, 1980.

James, E. T. *Notable American Women*, 1607 - 1950 Vol. III. Harvard University Press, 1971.

Marsh, John Stuart. *Man, Landscape and Recreation in Glacier National Park* 1856 - 1906. University of Calgary: PhD thesis, 1971.

Newhall, Beaumont. *This History of Photography.* New York: Museum of Modern Art, 1964.

Norman, Dorothy. *Alfred Stieglitz: An American Seer.* Aperture, 1973.

Outram, Sir James. *In the Heart of the Canadian Rockies.* New York: MacMillan, 1905.

Panzer, Mary. *Philadelphia Naturalistic Photography* 1865 - 1906. New Haven: Yale University Art Gallery, 1982.
———"Photographs from Nature." *Obscura* Vol. 1, No. 4, 1981.

Putnam, William Lowell. *The Great Glacier and its House.* New York: American Alpine Club, 1982.

Vaux, George X. "The Vaux Family's Scientific Pursuits" *Frontiers* Vol. III. Academy of Natural Sciences, Philadelphia, 1981 - 82.

Wheeler, A. O. *The Selkirk Range, British Columbia.* Ottawa, 1905.

Yochelson, Ellis L. *Charles Doolittle Walcott* 1850 - 1927 *A Biographical Memoir.* National Academy of Sciences, Washington, 1967.
———"C. D. Walcott." *Geotimes*, 1979.

Numerous articles and references from:
American Alpine Journal. The American Alpine Club.
Appalachia. The Appalachian Mountain Club.
Canadian Alpine Journal. The Alpine Club of Canada.
Journal of the Photographic Society of Philadelphia.

A Selection of Vaux family publications:

Vaux, George Jr. and William S. Jr. *Some Observations on the Illecillewaet and Asulkan Glaciers of British Columbia.* Proceedings of the Academy of Natural Sciences of Philadelphia, 1899.

———*Additional Observation on Glaciers in British Columbia.* Proceedings of the Academy of Natural Sciences of Philadelphia, 1899.

———*Observations made in 1900 on Glaciers in British Columbia.* Proceedings of the Academy of Natural Sciences of Philadelphia, 1901.

———*Observations made in 1906 on Glaciers in Alberta and British Columbia.* Proceedings of the Academy of Natural Sciences of Philadelphia, 1907.

———*Glaciers of the Canadian Rockies and Selkirks.* First edition, produced in conjunction with CPR, Bryn Mawr, Pennsylvania, 1900.

Vaux, Mary M. and George Jr. *Glaciers of the Canadian Rockies and Selkirks.* 2nd Edition 1911.

Vaux, Williams S. Jr. *The Canadian Pacific Railway, from Laggan to Revelstoke,* B.C. Proceedings of the Engineers Club of Philadelphia Vol. 17, No. 2, 1900.

———*Modern Glaciers: their movements and methods of observing them.* Proceedings of the Engineers Club of Philadelphia Vol. 24, No. 3, 1907.

Walcott, Mary Vaux. *The Glaciers of the Canadian Rockies and Selkirks.* 3rd edition, 1922.

———*North American Wild Flowers.* Washington, D.C.: the Smithsonian Institution, 1925.

———*Illustrations of North American Pitcher Plants.* Washington, D.C.: Smithsonian Institution, 1935.

Acknowledgements:

This publication and the companion exhibition would not have been possible without George and Henry Vaux. The family's photographic collection has been preserved in the Archives of the Canadian Rockies and made available to the public through their forethought and generosity.

A special debt of gratitude is due William Lowell Putnam, who is responsible for saving a copy of the *Scrapbook* before the original went astray. His book, *The Great Glacier and its House*, was of great assistance in preparing this publication.

I would like to thank Mary Panzer for sharing her knowledge of the Philadelphia photographic community and for her research assistance.

Nelson Vigneault deserves a special note for his excellent design and untiring efforts in the production of the duotone separations.

This book was, in fact, a co-operative venture involving most of the staff of the Whyte Foundation. I am indebted to all who have added their special expertise. Ted Hart, Brian Patton, and Jon Whyte imparted their editorial skills, proofreading abilities and essential research assistance; their patience and understanding as I battled the English language was amazing. Lena Goon (with a little help from Tessa Watt) not only managed to decipher most of the *Scrapbook* but was able to read my scrawl as well; she is also responsible for guiding the text material through the vagaries of the word-processor. Many thanks to Mary Andrews, Elizabeth Brown, and Carole Harmon for their proofreading abilities. Last, but hardly least, thanks to Craig Richards, the darkroom virtuoso.

Edward Cavell
Banff, April, 1983

Colophon:

Design:
Nelson Vigneault

Reproduction prints:
Craig Richards

Duotone separations:
United Graphic Services, Calgary, Alberta

Typesetting:
Duffoto Process Co. Ltd., Calgary, Alberta.

Printers:
D. W. Friesen and Sons Ltd., Altona, Manitoba.

Edward Cavell is Curator of Photography at the Whyte Foundation in Banff. He is author of *Journeys to the Far West* and *A Delicate Wilderness*, co-author of *Rocky Mountain Madness* with Jon Whyte and was photographic editor for *Calgary: An Illustrated History*.

Distributed by:
Altitude Publishing,
Box 490, Banff, Alberta TOL 0C0
(403) 762-4548

ISBN 0-920608-10-8